THE PICKERING MASTERS

CHRISTIANITY NOT AS OLD AS THE CREATION:
THE LAST OF DEFOE'S PERFORMANCES

T0347277

CHRISTIANITY NOT AS OLD AS THE CREATION:
THE LAST OF DEFOE'S PERFORMANCES

Edited by
G. A. Starr

Consulting Editors
W. R. Owens
P. N. Furbank

Routledge
Taylor & Francis Group

LONDON AND NEW YORK

First published 2012 by Pickering & Chatto (Publishers) Limited

2 Park Square, Milton Park, Abingdon, Oxfordshire OX14 4RN
52 Vanderbilt Avenue, New York, NY 10017

Routledge is an imprint of the Taylor & Francis Group, an informa business

First issued in paperback 2019

BRITISH LIBRARY CATALOGUING IN PUBLICATION DATA

Christianity not as old as the creation: the last of Defoe's performances. – (The
Pickering masters)
1. Christianity not as old as the creation – Authorship. 2. Tindal, Matthew,
1653?–1733. Christianity as old as the creation. 3. Defoe, Daniel, 1661?–1731.
New family instructor.
I. Series II. Starr, G. A. (George A.)
211.5–dc22

ISBN-13: 978-1-8489-3191-6 (hbk)
ISBN-13: 978-0-367-87613-5 (pbk)

Typeset by Pickering & Chatto (Publishers) Limited

CONTENTS

Acknowledgements   vii

Abbreviations   viii

Introduction   ix

Christianity Not as Old as the Creation   1

Explanatory Notes   63

Textual Notes   87

ACKNOWLEDGEMENTS

P. N. Furbank and W. R. Owens agreed to serve as Consulting Editors for this project; it has benefited from their detailed criticism and constructive suggestions, and I am once again very grateful for their generous assistance.

Forty years ago I dedicated a book to Fred Crews and Stanley Fish, because their presence as friends and colleagues made me happy and proud to be at Berkeley. They and my other great contemporaries have resigned or retired, but I am still optimistic about the English Department and glad to be part of it, thanks to brilliant young people like Joanna Picciotto and Geoffrey O'Brien. To them, with admiration and affection, I dedicate this edition.

In all notes and references, the place of publication is London unless otherwise indicated, and all post-1731 Defoe citations are from the 44-volume edition of his works (Pickering & Chatto, 2000–9), of which P. N. Furbank and W. R. Owens were the General Editors.

The following abbreviations are used throughout the Introduction and Explanatory Notes:

ABBREVIATIONS

Commentator	*The Commentator* (1720), in *Religious and Didactic Writings*, vol. 9, ed. P. N. Furbank (2007).
Compleat English Gentleman	*The Compleat English Gentleman* [1728–29], in *Religious and Didactic Writings*, vol. 10, ed. W. R. Owens (2007).
Complete English Tradesman I	*The Complete English Tradesman*, vol. 1 (1725), in *Religious and Didactic Writings*, vol. 7, ed. J. McVeagh (2007).
Compleat English Tradesman II	*The Compleat English Tradesman*, vol. II (1727), in *Religious and Didactic Writings*, vol. 8, ed. J. McVeagh (2007).
Conjugal Lewdness	*Conjugal Lewdness* (1727), in *Religious and Didactic Writings*, vol. 5, ed. L. Bellamy (2006).
Consolidator	*The Consolidator* (1705), in *Satire, Fantasy and Writings on the Supernatural*, vol. 3, ed. G. Sill (2005).
General History of Discoveries and Improvements	*A General History of Discoveries and Improvements, in Useful Arts* (1725–26), in *Writings on Travel, Discovery and History*, vol. 4, ed. P. N. Furbank (2001).
Family Instructor I	*The Family Instructor*, vol. I (1715), in *Religious and Didactic Writings*, vol. 1, ed. P. N. Furbank (2005).
Family Instructor II	*The Family Instructor*, vol. II (1718), in *Religious and Didactic Writings*, vol. 2, ed. P. N. Furbank (2005).
Farther Adventures	*The Farther Adventures of Robinson Crusoe* (1719), in *The Novels*, vol. 2, ed. W. R. Owens (2007).
Fortunate Mistress	*The Fortunate Mistress: or, a History of the Life and Vast Variety of Fortunes of Mademoiselle de Beleau, afterwards call'd the Countess of Wintselsheim, in Germany. Being the Person known by the Name of the Lady Roxana, in the Time of King Charles II* (1724), in *The Novels*, vol. 9, ed. P. N. Furbank (2009).
History and Reality of Apparitions	*An Essay on the History and Reality of Apparitions* (1727), in *Satire, Fantasy and Writings on the Supernatural*, vol. 8, ed. G. A. Starr (2005).
Jure Divino	*Jure Divino*, in *Satire, Fantasy and Writings on the Supernatural*, vol. 2, ed. P. N. Furbank (2003).

Letters written by a Turkish Spy	*A Continuation of Letters written by a Turkish Spy at Paris* (1718), in *Satire, Fantasy and Writings on the Supernatural*, vol. 5, ed. D. Blewett (2005).
Mere Nature Delineated	*Mere Nature Delineated: or, a Body without a Soul* (1726), in *Writings on Travel, Discovery and History*, vol. 5, ed. A. Wear (2002).
Moll Flanders	*The Fortunes and Misfortunes of the Famous Moll Flanders* (1722), ed. L. Bellamy, in *The Novels*, vol. 6 (2009).
New Family Instructor	*A New Family Instructor* (1727), in *Religious and Didactic Writings*, vol. 3, ed. W. R. Owens (2006).
New Voyage Round the World	*A New Voyage Round the World, by a Course never sailed before*, in *The Novels*, vol. 10, ed. J. McVeagh (2008).
Plan of the English Commerce	*A Plan of the English Commerce* (1728), in *Political and Economic Writings*, vol. 7, ed. J. McVeagh (2000).
Poetry	*The True-Born Englishman and Other Poems,* in *Satire, Fantasy and Writings on the Supernatural*, vol. 1, ed. W. R. Owens (2003).
Political History of the Devil	*The Political History of the Devil, as well Ancient as Modern* (1726), in *Satire, Fantasy and Writings on the Supernatural*, vol. 6, ed. J. Mullan (2004).
Religious Courtship	*Religious Courtship* (1722), in *Religious and Didactic Writings*, vol. 4, ed. G. A. Starr (2006).
Review	*Review*, vols.. I–VIII, ed. J. McVeagh (2002–10), vol. [IX], facs. ed. A. W. Secord (New York, 1938): cited by date of original issue, except that the *Supplement* is cited by month and page.
Robinson Crusoe	*The Life and Strange Surprizing Adventures of Robinson Crusoe* (1719), in *The Novels*, vol. 1, ed. W. R. Owens (2007).
Serious Reflections	*Serious Reflections during the Life and Surprising Adventures of Robinson Crusoe with his Vision of the Angelick World* (1720), in *The Novels*, vol. 3, ed. G. A. Starr (2008).
System of Magick	*A System of Magick; or, a History of the Black Art* (1727), in *Satire, Fantasy and Writings on the Supernatural*, vol. 7, ed. P. Elmer (2004).

INTRODUCTION

I. The Case for Attributing
Christianity Not as Old as the Creation to Daniel Defoe

There seems to me good reason for thinking that Defoe wrote *Christianity Not as Old as the Creation,* published in May 1730,[1] in answer to the Deist Matthew Tindal's *Christianity as Old as the Creation* of April 1730.[2] Tindal's book came to be known as 'the Deists' Bible', and it called forth dozens of replies in the 1730s,[3] but various features of Deism had already been provoking debate for decades. My evidence for Defoe's authorship of *Christianity Not as Old as the Creation* is entirely internal; according to Furbank and Owens's principles, the attribution should be classified as 'probable' rather than 'certain', as are many other items listed in their *Critical Bibliography.*[4] Biographical evidence does not give us much help over the ascription. In Defoe's letters there are suggestions that his health was bad, and that to avoid legal and financial ruin at the hands of actual or pretended creditors, he spent some of his final year on the move or in hiding, but at any rate not at home. About his domestic situation we know little, except that his protracted haggling with Henry Baker over the dowry of his daughter Sophia had been resolved; the no-longer-young couple was married, and exchanged renewed protestations of affection with Defoe. It would be natural to suppose that the more ill and harried he was, the less willing or able he would be to undertake and carry out a substantial polemical work.[5] Yet he had often been productive in unpromising circumstances, and amidst his tribulations he could conceivably have found Deist-bashing an invigorating therapeutic exercise. We know that in 1730 he was still actively engaged in business;[6] it seems that while there was life in him he could not give up buying and selling, and this may have been true of writing as well.[7] It is not hard to imagine that the bookseller Warner, alert to the *succès de scandale* of Tindal's book, approached Defoe (or that Defoe approached Warner) about producing a timely response. *Christianity as Old as the Creation* was published as a 432-

page, 15-shilling quarto volume in April, 1730, and *Christianity Not as Old as the Creation* appeared as a 95-page, 1-shilling octavo in May, 1730.[8] One of Defoe's early biographers remarks that 'When curiousness has contemplated such copiousness, such variety, and such excellence, it naturally inquires which was the last of De Foe's performances?'[9] Until now, a work that came out in February or March 1730 has been thought to be his final lifetime publication, *A Brief State of the Inland or Home Trade*.[10] If accepted as Defoe's, the present work would appear to have been the last of his performances.

The strongest single piece of internal evidence is the quotation, near the end of *Christianity Not as Old as the Creation*, of the following four lines of verse by Defoe:

> *If it should so fall out, as who can tell,*
> *But there may be a* GOD, *a* HEAVEN, *and* HELL,
> *Mankind had best consider well, for Fear*
> *'T should be too late when their Mistakes appear* (p. 58 below)

These lines are from Defoe's poem, *The Storm. An Essay*, which was published in 1704 together with *An Elegy on the Author of the True-Born-English-Man* (see *Poetry*, in *Satire, Fantasy and Writings on the Supernatural*, vol. 1, p. 289, ll. 248–51). The same lines were quoted by Defoe in *The Storm* (1704), Preface, sig. [A7]; twice in his *Serious Reflections* (in *Novels*, Vol. 3, pp. 117 and 264), and yet again in his 1726 work, the *Political History of the Devil* (in *Satire, Fantasy and Writings on the Supernatural*, vol. 6, p. 48). It is conceivable that a writer other than Defoe came across these lines in one or more of his works, and found them sufficiently memorable and apposite to quote them here. Yet it is hard to imagine them making as powerful an impression on anyone else as on Defoe himself, who had demonstrated his fondness for them by using them in four different works between 1704 and 1726 – and twice within one work, the *Serious Reflections*.

At a number of points there is a close correspondence between this work and Defoe's *New Family Instructor* of 1727. That book is a bold and sustained venture into controversial divinity, as its subtitle makes clear.[11] The present work is less expository, and on a smaller scale, but it belongs to the same genre. Abandoning the dialogue format, omitting the debates over Christ's status as God and Messiah, and expanding the critique of Deism beyond a vindication of Scripture, it is nevertheless the same *kind* of work, an attempt to defend sound belief against current fashions of unbelief. In both works, reformed Christianity is on the defensive; in both, the most immediate threat is from unbelief in its insidious modern guise of Deism, posing as a 'religion of nature' or a 'religion of reason'. *A New Family Instructor* spells out more fully the grounds for embracing the specific doctrines it advocates, such as the divinity of Christ, but both works are chiefly polemics against religious or irreligious positions held to be false and pernicious.

The resemblance goes well beyond a shared general purpose to a frequent and exact duplication of argument and language. For instance, one of Defoe's recurrent contentions is that the Deists aggrandize God's mercy at the expense of his justice. In *A New Family Instructor*, he asserts that 'They ... bring the Deity ... under such Regulations and Restrictions, that they scarce allow him to be a GOD at all. They will have him be so good, so merciful, so beneficent, that he cannot be Just' (*Religious and Didactic Writings*, vol. 3, p. 204). 'What kind of a God must we make of him', the present author asks, '*Who is so merciful, he can't be just?*' (p. 42 below), and he declares, 'It is evident his Vengeance against Offenders is often declared with Terror, *the wrath of God is reveal'd from Heaven against all unrighteousness*, Rom. i. 18' (p. 42 below). In *A New Family Instructor,* to combat the Deists' view that God looks on sinners 'with Pity ... and Compassion, but no Anger and Displeasure, which is below his Infinite Greatness, and the Sovereignty of his Mercy', Defoe cites the same verse, and insists that God is 'angry, and will ... deal in the utmost Vengeance and Resentment against the guilty Sinner, unless he repents' (*Religious and Didactic Writings*, vol. 3, p. 205).

Often the two books make the same point in identical terms. Here the author claims that quibbling Deists 'will find the very Image of God stampt upon every part of [the Bible] ... with a visible Signature of the Divine Authority'; that throughout there are 'eminent Signatures of the high Original of the Scriptures' (pp. 46, 48 below); and he asks, 'Are not these Marks of a Divine Impression?' (p. 48 below). In *A New Family Instructor*, the Deists are said to 'deny its [the Bible's] being of Divine Original, and ... of Divine Authority', but the father's response is that 'it has all the Marks of Divine Impression upon it that can be thought of ... One immediately sees the Stamp of his Divine Authority upon every Part of it' (*Religious and Didactic Writings*, vol. 3, p. 207). Further similarities between the two books are detailed in the Explanatory Notes.

There are many significant parallels between *Christianity Not as Old as the Creation* and other works known to be by Defoe. The list that follows is arranged by page number in the present edition.

'Men are very fond of distinguishing themselves, not into good Principles but out of them' (p. 6 below):

Compare *A Letter to Mr. How* (1701), p. 15: 'such is the Subtilty and Nicety of Sophistical Reasonings, that Men may almost Distinguish themselves into, and out of any Opinion; and some People ... too often lose both Themselves and their Religion in the Labyrinths of Words'. In *The Consolidator*, in *Satire, Fantasy and Writings on the Supernatural*, vol. 3, p. 94, Defoe mocks those whose casuistical 'distinguishing Power' enables them to 'distinguish themselves into or out of any Opinion, either in Religion, Politicks or Civil Right'. Compare also *A New Family Instructor*, in *Religious and Didactic Writings*, vol. 3, p. 203: 'It is an unhappy Pleasure some People take in endeavouring to argue themselves not into good Principles, but out of them'; 'A Vision of the Angelick World', in *Serious Reflections*, in *Novels*, vol. 3, p. 260: 'instead of Reasoning themselves into good Principles of Religion, they really reason'd themselves out of all Religion'. Moll Flanders says that her old 'Governess' 'reason'd me out of my Reason': see *Moll Flanders*, in *Novels*, vol. 6, p. 150.

'to say *Natural Religion* is indeed to say nothing, or nothing to the Purpose' (p. 7 below); see also p. 36 below, 'To say ... is saying Nothing'; p. 61 below, 'To say ... is to say nothing':

This expression is found often in Defoe's works. See *The Manufacturer* (22 December 1720), 'to say ... is to say nothing, or nothing to the purpose'. In the *Review*, Defoe says that 'to talk of ... had been to say nothing to the purpose' (1 January 1706); that 'To say ... is to say nothing, or at least to say nothing, but what shall further illustrate what I am upon' (28 March 1706); that 'To say ... *is saying nothing*' (4 May 1706); that if you do ... 'you have done nothing at all, *or nothing to the purpose*, which is the same thing' (4 June 1706).

'If Reason ... is infinite in Prescience ... then Reason is GOD' (p. 9 below):

In *A System of Magick*, in *Satire, Fantasy and Writings on the Supernatural*, vol. 7, p. 282, Defoe challenges the view that spirits can see into the future; this would require of them 'an infinite Prescience, by which they must every one of them know ... the Desires, Wishes, Fears, Terrors, and Hopes of ... all People whatever, in all Places and Times, ... and to do so would be to be absolutely and essentially God'.

'See my Lord *Rochester* upon this Subject in his Satyr upon Man.
Reason which fifty times for one does err!' (p. 10 below):

The reference here is to 'A Satyre Against Reason and Mankind', l. 11: see *The Works of John Wilmot Earl of Rochester*, ed. Harold Love (Oxford, 1998), p. 57. Defoe cites this poem in the *History and Reality of Apparitions*, in *Satire, Fantasy and Writings on the Supernatural*, vol. 8, p. 45, and twice in the *Serious Reflections*, in *Novels*, Vol. 3, pp. 73, 131.

'Tho' Scripture is not allow'd in Evidence ... yet we may bring Allusions from Scripture History' (p. 12 below):

In *A System of Magick*, in *Satire, Fantasy and Writings on the Supernatural*, vol. 7, p. 103, Defoe says parenthetically and wryly of Scripture, 'I hope that Book, when 'tis taken as a History only, may obtain Credit enough to be brought in Evidence'. Cf. also p. 146: '*The Scripture*, whether our good Friends that read Books in this Age will bear with our quoting it in Matters of Religion or no, yet is generally allow'd to be a tolerable good History. Nay ... it must be allow'd to be the most ancient History, and the Writing from which all other Authorities take their Rise'. In the *History and Reality of Apparitions*, in *Satire, Fantasy and Writings on the Supernatural*, vol. 8, p. 75, Defoe refers to Scripture, 'which I must allow to be an authentick Document, whatever the Reader may please to do, 'till a History more authentick, and of better Authority may be produc'd in the Room of it'; he also says that the biblical testimony regarding apparitions is 'so plain and unquestionable ... that they who dispute it, must not only doubt of the Divinity of Scripture, but must dispute its being an authentick History; which its Enemies will hardly deny' (p. 77). A similar distinction is drawn in *A New Family Instructor*, in *Religious and Didactic Writings*, vol. 3, p. 206: 'though they will not allow Scripture Doctrine, they cannot deny Scripture-History; they cannot deny the Facts related in Scripture, nor can they bring any Evidence against the Fidelity of the Relations, or of the Relator'.

'capable of acting upon Futurity, and upon Spirit, in a very extraordinary manner' (p. 14 below):

See 'A Vision of the Angelick World', in *Serious Reflections*, in *Novels*, vol. 3, p. 236, 'the Soul of Man is capable to act strangely upon the Invisibles in Nature, and upon Futurity'; cf. also p. 256: 'Matter may act upon material Objects, and so the Understanding or Sense of a Brute may act upon visible Objects, but Matter cannot act upon immaterial Things, and so the Eye of a Beast cannot see a Spirit, or the Mind of a Brute act upon Futurity, Eternity, and the sublime Things of a State to come'.

'to hide himself among a few Bushes from the Search of, INFINITE! and then to cover his Nakedness from the sight of Beasts' (p. 26 below):

In the *Political History of the Devil*, in *Satire, Fantasy and Writings on the Supernatural*, Vol. 6, p. 101, Defoe represents Adam and Eve after the fall 'skulking with a sordid Flight, / Among the Bushes from the *Infinite*', and 'With senseless Labour tagging Fig-Leaf-Vests, / To hide their Bodies from the sight of Beasts'; he had used these lines earlier (with 'senseless' instead of 'sordid') in book 7, ll. 112–15 of *Jure Divino,* in *Satire, Fantasy and Writings on the Supernatural*, vol. 2, pp. 219–20.

'*Nulla gens tam barbara quæ nescit esse Deum*' (p. 26 below):

In the *Serious Reflections*, in *Novels*, vol. 3, p. 151, Defoe gives this in abbreviated form: 'the Profession of Religion ... I find almost in every Nation, *Nulla gens tam barbara*'.

'the thing ... is as needless as it is impossible to know' (p. 30 below):

See the *Review* (17 May 1711), 'Whether ... or ... is as needless, as it is impossible to know'; see also the *Political History of the Devil*, in *Satire, Fantasy and Writings on The Supernatural*, vol. 6, p. 286, where Defoe says the way the devil will be tormented 'I take to be as needless to us as 'tis impossible to know'; cf. also the 'weak and imperfect Guesses' in the same sentence with the 'crude Guesses' in the present passage.

[Adam] 'talk'd like a Fool' (p. 40 below):

In his facetious account of the fall of Adam and Eve in the *Political History of the Devil*, in *Satire, Fantasy and Writings on the Supernatural*, vol. 6, pp. 101–4, Defoe says 'what Fools they both acted like', scoffs that 'all the Knowledge they attain'd to' by eating the apple was 'only to know that they were Fools', and dismisses Adam's defence: 'the Fool pleads faint, for forfeit Life'. On p. 74, he had cited 'a certain author, whose name ... I conceal' – but whose ironic stress on Adam's folly sounds like Defoe himself – as making Eve say to Adam, '*eat and be a stupid fool no longer ... What ails the* SOT? *... take it, you Fool, and eat ... if you don't, I'll go and cut down the Tree, and you shall never eat any of it at all, and you shall be still a fool, and be governed by your wife for ever*'.

'*Who is so merciful, he can't be just?*' (p. 42 below):

The source of this verse has not been traced; it may be Defoe's, but in any case it expresses an idea prominent in his critiques of Deism. In addition to the passage already quoted from *A New Family Instructor*, see the *Serious*

Reflections, in *Novels*, Vol. 3, p.101, where Defoe refers to 'a fine well bred good natur'd Gentleman like Deity, that cannot have the Heart to damn any of his Creatures to an Eternal Punishment'. In *A System of Magick*, in *Satire, Fantasy and Writings on the Supernatural*, Vol. 7, p. 182, Defoe maintains that the Deists divest God of 'all Resentment against the vilest Offences: robbing him of the Power of Rewards and Punishments, and making him so good, so kind and gracious, that they do not leave him room to be Just'. The line-ending formula '*he can't be just*' occurs in book 6, l. 463 of *Jure Divino*, in *Satire, Fantasy and Writings on the Supernatural*, vol. 2, p. 212.

'a wonderful Concurrence of Circumstance' (p. 47):
    See the *Review* (30 May 1706): 'I should think we were wanting to our Judgments, if we were blind to the Connexion and Concurrence of Circumstances and Providences in the World'; see also *Review* (19 November 1706): 'tho' I take great Notice of the Concurrence of Circumstances, and the strange Revolution of Times, yet does my Observation of Days lead to no Superstition, or at all bind up the Providence of GOD to such Circumstances'.

'the Devil, whose Power of Prediction, some have suggested to be great, tho'' ... there is nothing of that kind in his Power' (p. 47 below):
    See *A New Family Instructor*, in *Religious and Didactic Writings*, vol. 3, pp. 213, 215: 'the Devil knows nothing before-hand ... the *Devil* has no Power of Prediction, no Fore-knowledge of Things to come'. See also the *History and Reality of Apparitions*, in *Satire, Fantasy and Writings on the Supernatural*, vol. 8, p. 76, 'I have no reason to believe that Satan knows any thing of Futurity'; the *Political History of the Devil*, in *Satire, Fantasy and Writings on the Supernatural*, vol. 6, p. 117; and *A System of Magick*, in *Satire, Fantasy and Writings on the Supernatural*, vol. 7, pp. 99, 204.

'his Justice in pursuing the Murtherer, often bringing him even to detect himself, and be the Instrument of his own just Punishment' (p. 52 below); see also p. 60 below, 'the guilty Soul ... has no Rest Night or Day, till he even detects himself':
    For Defoe's view that those 'guilty of any atrocious Villany' are often 'oblig'd to Discover it' themselves through a 'Necessity of Nature', see *Moll Flanders*, in *Novels*, vol. 6, p. 262. In the *History and Reality of Apparitions*, in *Satire, Fantasy and Writings on the Supernatural*, vol. 8, pp. 112–19, a man guilty of murder imagines he sees his victim in court, is terrified, and confesses his crime; cf. n. 160, pp. 332–3. See *Review, A Supplement to the*

Advice from the Scandal Club, November 1704; *Jure Divino*, book 3, ll. 27–40, in *Satire, Fantasy and Writings on the Supernatural*, vol. 2, p. 128. Defoe's youthful 'Historical Collecions' contains the story of a man executed fifteen years after he had committed a murder, driven to confess because 'the horrour of his Conscience so terrefyed him'.

'frequent Examples, where the Crime has been seen in the very Punishment' (p. 52 below):
   See *Serious Reflections*, in *Novels*, vol. 3, pp. 188–9: 'when visible Punishments follow visible Crimes, who can refrain confessing the apparent Direction of supreme Justice? When Concurrence of Circumstances directs to the Cause, Men that take no Notice ... openly contemn Heaven ... Men may ... see the Crime ... in the divine Resentment, may read the Sin in the Punishment'. Several characters in the *Family Instructor II*, in *Religious and Didactic Writings*, vol. 2, are said to be able to read their sins in their punishments: see pp. 13, 149, 156. In the *Commentator* (16 September 1720), in *Religious and Didactic Writings*, vol. 9, p. 309, 'The *sin is known by the* Punishment'; in *Religious Courtship*, in *Religious and Didactic Writings*, vol. 4, p. 187, a rueful father acknowledges that 'Providence seems to shew me my Sin, by my Punishment'. In the *Political History of the Devil*, in *Satire, Fantasy and Writings on the Supernatural*, vol. 6, p. 73, Heaven is said to have made Eve's 'entire subjection to her husband be a part of the Curse, that she might read her sin in the punishment'; cf. also the *Review* (9 June 1713).

'hurried down the stream of their Affections' (p. 53 below):
   See 'hurries us down the Stream of our Affections', *Serious Reflections*, in *Novels*, vol. 3, p. 129; 'hurry'd down the Stream of their own Affections', 'A Vision of the Angelick World', in the *Serious Reflections*, in *Novels*, Vol. 3, p. 241. See also 'to be hurry'd down the Stream of the Affections', in *Conjugal Lewdness*, in *Religious and Didactic Writings*, vol. 5, p. 210; 'hurried down the Stream of our own Desires', in *Farther Adventures*, in *Novels*, vol 2, p. 126. In the *Political History of the Devil*, in *Satire, Fantasy and Writings on the Supernatural*, vol. 6, p. 283, our 'Affections' are said to be 'possess'd', so that the soul is 'hurried down the Stream to embrace low and base Objects'.

'to raze out the fear of God from the Minds of Men' (p. 55 below):
   See the *Political History of the Devil*, in *Satire, Fantasy and Writings on the Supernatural*, vol. 6, p. 132: 'the *Devil* did not immediately rase out the Notion of Religion and of a God from the Minds of Men'; cf. also *A System of Magick*, in *Satire, Fantasy and Writings on the Supernatural*, Vol. 7, p. 179:

it requires hellish magic to 'raze out the Impressions of a GOD from the Soul of Man'.

'the Gust of your own Desires' (p. 59 below):

A 'gust' is primarily a taste, relish, or inclination, but Defoe often uses it to mean a keen (and usually a culpable) one, as in 'a strong powerful Gust to these Delights' and 'Satan's Gust of doing Evil', in 'A Vision of the Angelick World', in the *Serious Reflections,* in *Novels,* vol. 3, pp. 243 and 259. The present near-tautological phrase is a favorite of Defoe's. In *Conjugal Lewdness,* in *Religious and Didactic Writings,* vol. 5, p. 192, he condemns those who gratify a 'Gust of vitious Desire', and also refers to 'a Gust of general desire' (p. 59), a 'gust of Appetite' (p. 77) and 'the Gust of Inclination' (p. 157). In the *Family Instructor I,* in *Religious and Didactic Writings,* vol. 1, p. 122, he speaks of people 'abandon'd to the Gust of their own Inclinations'; the drunken gentleman Moll Flanders meets in Bartholomew Fair has 'a wicked Gust in his Inclination', in *Novels,* vol. 6, p. 189; cf. also 'the wicked Gust of an unbridled perverse Inclination' in the *Family Instructor II,* in *Religious and Didactic Writings,* vol. 2, p. 85, and 'this Gust of their greedy Appetite' in *A New Voyage Round the World,* in *Novels,* vol. 10, p. 239. When other writers use 'gust' in close proximity to 'inclination' or to 'appetite', they usually join the two terms as virtual synonyms, as in 'Gust and Inclination' (John Tillotson, *Works,* 2nd edn, 3 vols (1717), vol. 2, p. 190), and in 'Gust or Appetite' (Jeremy Taylor, *The Rule and Exercises of Holy Dying,* 24th edn (1727), p. 39).

'the vindictive Attribute of God' (p. 60 below; repeated two paragraphs later):

The phrase 'vindictive attribute' occurs in the *Serious Reflections,* in *Novels,* vol. 3, p. 166; I have found no other instance of it.

In conclusion, I know of no positive external evidence linking Defoe to *Christianity Not as Old as the Creation,* nor do I know of any negative external evidence, such as attributions of the work to others. As to negative internal evidence, Defoe's writings do not, to my knowledge, explicitly repudiate or implicitly contradict positions taken here; or to put it the other way around, nothing in the present work seems to me to rule him out as author. Positive internal evidence is abundant and significant. This book contains many of Defoe's favorite (and idiosyncratic) ideas, phrases and allusions. It displays close similarities of purpose and argument to Defoe's writings on religious topics. Most notably, it quotes Defoe's two favorite authors (Rochester and himself), in contexts where others would be unlikely to invoke them. The case for Defoe's probable authorship therefore seems quite strong.

II. Defoe and Deism

The Circumstances of Publication of *Christianity Not as Old as the Creation*

The *occasion* of this book was Tindal's *Christianity as Old as the Creation* and its instant notoriety.[12] The ironic cleverness of Tindal's title may not be obvious to modern readers. Ostensibly, Tindal is lauding Christianity. Instead of being a historically and geographically localized movement, which emerged at a specific moment in a narrowly Middle Eastern setting, Christianity is represented as timeless and universal, co-extensive with creation itself. Or so Tindal appears to suggest; and in one sense this is indeed what he maintains – but with a crucial, devastating caveat: namely, that what is *true* in Christianity is as old as the creation. With this qualification, he can proceed to narrow the truth of Christianity to what it shares with the religion of nature, which has been available to mankind in all times and places. As Tindal and other Deists define it, the religion of nature consists of a few fundamental doctrines, e.g. that God exists, that he is perfectly reasonable and benevolent, and that he demands nothing irksome or unreasonable from mankind. All other dogmas and creeds, in whatever religion they have become enshrined, are held to be extraneous if not contrary to the religion of nature, and are imputed to the self-serving efforts of priestcraft.

Behind its seeming supportiveness toward Christianity, Tindal's title thus disguises a basic and far-reaching antagonism. The timeless, universal truths of Christianity are made to seem minimal, incidental elements amidst a mass of dubious and pernicious accretions. Its truths (such as they are) are identical with those of all other religions, since they consist only of principles that supposedly force themselves on man's unaided reason, whatever his experience. The implications for Christianity are doubly deflationary. First, it is deprived of its uniqueness: whatever truth it possesses, it shares with similar cults the world over, most of which Christians are apt to derogate as pagan or primitive. Second, Christianity has many features – most notably, revelation – other than those based on natural religion. But besides resembling the legends and superstitions of other religions, these other features are treated by Tindal and other Deists as at best superfluous and at worst fatal to sound religion. Ultimately, what might be called the golden-rule portion of Christianity, which happens to correspond with the teachings of Confucius, Socrates and other wise pagans, is retained and praised. All the rest is disregarded or discredited, and the task of reduction is carried out most effectively not through frontal attacks but indirectly, by satirizing aspects of supernaturalism and priestcraft that obviously stand for Christianity.

The *object* of the present book, however, is not so much to refute Tindal as to challenge Deism in general. There are passing references to Tindal's text (pp. 17, 20, 25), and an allusion to the title of one other Deistic book (p. 13 and Explanatory n. 32). Beyond this, the positions being attacked are not traced to specific authors or works, but ascribed to the Deists collectively, who are reviled as 'the Enemies of God', 'the Infidels of this Age', the *Free-Thinkers* of the Age' and 'these new Religion-makers' (pp. 5, 14, 9, 28), as if these roles are played equally by all Deists. Despite his opprobrious epithets for the Deists as a group, the present author does not reduce them to mere men of straw, but grapples with the substance and implications of various Deistic tenets.

The topic of Deism becomes prominent in Defoe's works of the 1720s, although as early as 1706, he had quoted sympathetically a Scottish indictment of the current state of English religion:

> Many of those [in England], who most set up for Knowledge, Parts, Wit and Sense, above their Neighbours, are hid or open Owners of Deism, prefering blind Natural, to the Heavenly Light of reveal'd Religion, and treating in Ridicule the Holy Scriptures, Regeneration, the Imputed Righteousness of Christ, and the Fundamental Doctrine of three Persons in the God-head, both in Discourses and publick Writing, without any publick Search or Censure.[13]

Over the decades, Defoe and his fictional characters had often made self-effacing gestures when writing about religious topics: 'Divinity is not my Talent, nor ever like to be my Profession'; 'my Business is not Preaching'; 'I am not given to preach'; 'I ... am but a very mean Expositor of Texts'; ''tis no Business of mine, to enter upon the Interpretation of Scripture Difficulties'.[14] But by the time of *A New Family Instructor*, this note of seeming diffidence is replaced by an air of considerable assurance; proof-texts are marshalled as if their cumulative force were irresistible. The present work is similarly assertive, brandishing abundant and apposite Scriptural evidence even though its validity is the very thing the Deists deny. Beginning with the *Serious Reflections during the Life and Surprising Adventures of Robinson Crusoe* (1720), Defoe repeatedly treats Deism, freethinking, and scepticism as interchangeable preludes to (or masks for) outright atheism.[15] His previously-known writing on the Deists challenges the assumptions, principles and goals he thinks they have in common, and seldom cites texts or analyses passages. One can speculate as to which writers provoked his indignation, yet for the most part he avoids identifying individual Deists, or focusing on actual specimens of their work, emphasizing instead the threat they collectively pose to Christianity.[16]

Truth, Error and their Consequences

It is characteristic of Defoe to weigh competing belief-systems in terms of the behaviour of their adherents. In the *Serious Reflections*, Christianity is defended against other religions not only for being in sole possession of saving truth, but for making its practitioners better and more humane.[17] In *Christianity as Old as the Creation*, Tindal makes contrary claims; he agrees with Samuel Clarke that 'Man is naturally ... full of Benevolence, Pity, and Tenderness', but asserts that 'the Christian Religion ... has transform'd this social, and benign Creature, into one fierce, and cruel'.[18] Similarly provocative is Tindal's citation of 'Monsieur *Leibnitz*', who 'in comparing the Christians at present, with the Infidels of *China*, does not scruple to give the preference to the latter, in relation to all *moral Virtues*'.[19] In the present work, actual practice is used as a test of doctrinal validity: the conclusions reached are the opposite of Tindal's, but the same as Defoe's: 'Certainly, that Religion which has a real Tendency to make the World worse, and not better, cannot claim to be the best, and truest Religion' (p. 54 below). The lines are drawn sharply: Deism is represented as fostering licence, Christianity as promoting virtue. In many such passages, the *consequences* of beliefs are treated as a decisive gauge of their validity.

The Pascalian wager, introduced twice in this work (pp. 49, 58 below), functions the same way: that is, it shifts the focus of discussion away from the inherent truth of Christian doctrine to the relative risks of accepting or rejecting it. In his defender-of-the-faith mode, Defoe frequently uses this kind of argument, as if the practical consequences of holding or denying some doctrine are reliable tests of its soundness. When he is discussing his own behaviour or that of sympathetic fictional characters, he tends to reject such reasoning, and treats overt deeds as limited and misleading evidence of people's real characters or beliefs. But when his adversaries are the ones behaving badly, he finds it legitimate to infer that they act from wrong principles or none at all. The present work employs this strategy against the Deists, whose indulgence in 'all manner of Levities' and 'the worst of Vices' is said to be owing to 'their debauch'd Reasonings' on religious subjects (see p. 53 below).

The related view that rewards and punishments have a central and legitimate part to play in Christian doctrine is also very prominent in this work.

The Deists refuse to believe that God would be so harsh as to punish sinners eternally; they maintain that he is all 'Goodness and Beneficence', and that 'all thoughts of his Anger and Resentment, be the Cause ever so great, are unworthy of God' (p. 54 below). This notion provokes the author's indignation: to him, 'the vindictive Attribute of God',[20] his vengeance, is perfectly compatible with, and a necessary complement to, his 'infinite Goodness'. 'What kind of a God must we make of him', he asks, '*Who is so merciful, he can't be just?*' (p. 42 below). In several works of the 1720s, Defoe scoffs at the Deists on identical grounds.[21]

Traditional doctrines regarding hell and eternal torment were losing their credibility and monitory force for many Christians.[22] More generally, rewards and punishments were being questioned as grounds for moral choice by those who thought that such sanctions encourage prudential selfishness rather than sympathy or benevolence.[23] The Deists were vigorous spokesmen for this position. According to them, a system of rewards and punishments rules out love of God, because we can't love what we fear. To keep people in line by mere hope of reward and fear of punishment can succeed, as it clearly does with trained animals and brutish humans, but the resulting order cannot be regarded as moral, since it is based not on principled choice but on selfish, more or less instinctive desires to maximize one's own pleasure and minimize pain. Such a scheme is unworthy of the dignity or generosity of either God or mankind, for whom the good cannot be narrow self-seeking, but benevolent action in keeping with the dictates of reason and the laws of nature.

The present author expresses no such misgivings. To arouse in readers a dread of incurring God's wrath, here or hereafter, is one of his chief objectives in the latter part of the book, where unbelievers and evildoers are threatened with divine punishment. The Deists 'exalt the Mercy and Goodness of God' to the point of supposing that 'we may act as we please, and that he will not take Vengeance upon us, if we sin against him' (p. 53 below). The doctrinal error of the Deists has dire practical consequences, which dominate the rhetoric of the Appendix. In Defoe's novels, heroes and heroines violate various legal and ethical norms, but except for Roxana, most of them manage to escape the punishments that (as they themselves recognize) they deserve. In his conduct manuals, however, such as *The Family Instructor*, misdeeds are penalized drastically, thus demonstrating that God is not a detached observer, but an active avenger of transgressions. The connection between the act and its aftermath is often so close as to enable the guilty party 'to read the Crime in its Punishment', and to see in it the hand of divine justice.[24] The reader is expected to do so as well.

These themes are prominent in the present work: for instance, in allusions to 'the open Discoveries of Divine Vengeance upon desperate Criminals, and how it is so pointed, and so tim'd, that we have frequent Examples, where the Crime has been seen in the very Punishment' (p. 52 below). The principle that sins and crimes can be 'read' in their punishments is not directed specifically against Tindal's *Christianity as Old as the Creation*, but it is germane to the broader contention that the Deists have a false and pernicious notion of God, aggrandizing his mercy at the expense of his justice. At a time when many philosophers and divines preferred a more genial image of the deity, the present author strenuously affirms God's 'vindictive Attribute'. His emphasis on divine justice reveals a certain affinity with the punitive, fire-and-brimstone Calvinism of Jonathan Edwards's sermon on *Sinners in the Hands of an Angry God* (Boston, 1741). True, Edwards contemplates the endless sufferings of the damned with a zestful intensity that is absent from the present book and from the writings of Defoe, who asserts but does not revel (as does Edwards) in the prospect of the eternal punishment of the wicked. Nevertheless Defoe resembles Edwards, and differs from many of his English contemporaries, in averring that hell exists, and that it awaits evildoers; he sidesteps unprofitable speculation as to its location and exact nature, but is in no doubt as to its reality, and both its practical and theological importance. Practically, he regards hell as a vital deterrent from sin and spur to timely conversion and repentance. Theologically, he sees hell (no less than heaven) as validating divine justice, which might be open to sceptical questioning if its scope were limited to the distribution of rewards and punishments in this life.

It goes without saying that Defoe does not regard God's vindictiveness as spiteful, petty or malicious, but he does not try to drain it of anger. In fact, he suggests that God's punitiveness springs not merely from his sense of justice, but also from the wrath provoked by human violation of his commandments. According to the Deists, God 'must be infinitely Wise, Good, Righteous, Holy and Just'; but according to the wise father in *A New Family Instructor*, 'if he is infinitely holy and pure, he cannot look on Sin, which is in its Nature all Impurity and Corruption, without Abhorrence; and by Consequence of his Justice, he must look on the Sinner with *Resentment* and *Displeasure*: How else can he be Just?'[25] But his daughter responds, 'No, no, they [the Deists] will not allow that, they say he looks on them with Pity indeed and Compassion, but no Anger and Displeasure, which is below his

Infinite Greatness, and the Sovereignty of his Mercy'. Told by his daughter that they regard it as 'against Reason to argue otherwise', the father responds 'And we say 'tis against *Revelation* to argue so: *The Wrath of God is revealed from* Heaven *against all Ungodliness and Unrighteousness of Men*, Rom. I. 18'. But the discussion has reached an impasse: as the daughter exclaims, 'O! Sir, they despise all *Revelation* and all *Scripture*'. For Defoe, as for the father in *A New Family Instructor*, the angry God of the Old Testament remains wrathful in the New, and such explicit, emphatic texts constitute incontrovertible evidence of God's nature and actions. For the Deists, anything attributed to God in the Bible that does not fit their own conception of an entirely reasonable deity must, they argue, be a false notion inserted in the text by designing priests, to legitimate and maintain their control over a fearful and superstitious populace. To suppose that God could be subject to such an emotion or passion strikes the Deists as a Judaeo-Christian derogation of his dignity, an imputation to him of an all-too-human weakness. The Deists, holding that if God exists he must be perfect, treat wrath as a failing even in humans, and thus inconceivable as a divine attribute.[26] Tindal quotes approvingly Shaftesbury's sentiments on this subject:

> If there be a Religion that teaches the Adoration and Love of a God, whose Character it is to be captious, and of high Resentment, subject to Wrath and Anger, furious, revengeful, and revenging himself, when offended, on others than those who gave the Offence ... 'Tis evident that such a Religion ... must of Necessity raise even an Approbation and Respect towards the Vices of this Kind, and breed a suitable Disposition, a capricious, partial, revengeful, and deceitful Temper.[27]

By 'such a Religion', of course, Shaftesbury means traditional Christianity. Tindal himself deplores those who blacken the 'Character of the Deity' by 'imput[ing] such Actions to him, as make him resemble the worst of Beings, and so run into downright *Demonism*'.[28] The Deists' concern with an afterlife chiefly takes the form of denying as barbarous the notion of eternal punishment. The very existence of hell, either as a place or a state, is challenged by them, first of all because subjecting mankind to endless torment would go against the essential mercifulness of a perfect God, and 'make him resemble the worst of Beings', his enemy Satan. Furthermore, Tindal and others argue that any punishment meted out by a benevolent God must be temporary and corrective in nature, designed to qualify people for their ultimate well-being. To torture them forever would therefore violate the meliorative function that any punishment administered by him must serve. And it would violate divine justice itself, given the apparent imbalance between any human transgression and its perpetual, unremitting punishment.

Both the Deists and Defoe think God must be perfect, but they have different ideals of perfection. The Deists, valuing reason as man's highest quality, posit a god who epitomizes pure reasonableness, and then elaborate some concomitant attributes of such a deity. But their definition of God also unfolds by a process of elimination: they strip away from the supreme being whatever traits they regard as flaws or weaknesses in humanity, leaving him with only those attributes that they deem consistent with (their idea of) reasonableness. What they cast aside are many of the traits that humanize, for better and for worse, the Biblical God – or at any rate, the God of the Old Testament and the Pauline epistles: namely, the passions, often of a somber hue, that run so strongly in the Scriptural God and his chosen people alike. To the Deists such a god, at once deplorable and absurd, must be not only a human invention, but the contrivance of a thoroughly sinister priesthood. The Deists thus seize upon some problematic features of the traditional Christian conception of God, and in the course of the Eighteenth Century their view of this matter was to prevail, insofar as a dour Augustinian and Calvinist image of the deity gave way to their more genial one. But Defoe and others argued that by trying to minimize or deny the place of passion in the divine nature, the Deists were reviving the cold, distant, impersonal deity postulated by the Stoics and Epicureans of antiquity, a deity whose role either in creation or in the ongoing management of the universe was reduced (as it seemed to the orthodox) to the point of nonexistence. In other words, the Deists might claim to believe in a god, but the function of such a god in making or running the world was negligible. He was prevented from having brought the world into being by the impossibility (as Epicureans had long maintained) of creating matter out of nothing. And he was prevented (by the reason-bound laws of nature) from intervening in the conduct of a universe once it was set in motion. In short, the god of the Deists had little or nothing to do.[29]

To discredit this theology as Epicureanism and atheism, defenders of Christianity drew on various modes of argument. At the time, the most influential was probably the set of strategies known as 'physico-theology', which sought to demonstrate that the universe – a 'book of nature' now more legible than ever thanks to microscopes and telescopes – must have been created and continues to be actively, providentially governed by just such a God as has also revealed himself in that other book, the Scriptures which he dictated or inspired. Defoe was in sympathy with those who regarded the 'new science' as confirming rather than calling in question religious truth, but his own way of dealing with the challenge of Deism was on the whole more conservative. According to the Deists, in a universe ruled by reason (such as ours), the laws of nature are uniform and constant, and by interpreting our experience of these laws in the light of reason, man can arrive at truth. Although much may remain to be discovered about these laws, this is the only method by which man can hope to gain solid knowledge, and at various times and places throughout history, wise men have in fact succeeded in figuring out for themselves all they need to know about their relationships with God and one another. On this sanguine view, revelation is at best redundant, since it can do no more than reiterate truths that man is fully capable of learning without supernatural assistance, and at worst pernicious and illusory in form as well as content. That is, revelation purports to impart truths by means that circumvent our ordinary way of acquiring knowledge through experience and reason, and it represents events as occurring – e.g. miracles – that violate all we know through experience and reason. In the former category, the Deists ridicule the idea of Greco-Roman divinities communicating with humans through soothsayers, oracles, sibyls and the like, although the object of their satire is ultimately not pagan antiquity but Scripture. In the latter category, the Deists mock the fabulous legends of heathen and primitive religions, but their real if unstated target is again Biblical, the miraculous material in both Old and New Testaments.

The Appendix purports to be '*Affectionately address'd to the Youth of this Age*': its intention may be charitable, yet its tone seems more dour than affectionate. The father in *A New Family Instructor* expresses many of the same ideas, often in the same words, but he holds the sympathetic interest of his children by bringing 'as much of it as he could into Story', by explaining everything 'in a familiar Way, easy to be receiv'd', and by his 'pleasant agreeable Way of Talking'.[30] Here these engaging qualities are less in evidence; the authorial voice is solemn, but not unrelievedly so. At one point Charles II is quoted as doubting '*That God who is a gracious and beneficent Being, will be so severe as to punish eternally for a few out of the way Pleasures*' (p. 38 below). Anticipating the Deists' cynical attempts to deny God's justice by emphasizing his mercy, the royal libertine reduces his own flagrant sins to '*a few out of the way Pleasures*'. Like the allusion to Rochester elsewhere (p. 10 below), the reference here to Charles II is the kind of gesture that a clerical author would be likely to eschew as indecorous in the midst of a serious theological argument. Defoe, however, often introduces half-earnest, half-jesting touches of worldly wit unexpectedly. In his late-Metaphysical mode (more pronounced in his religious poetry than in his prose), the bolder and more far-fetched the allusion, the better. To be sure, Charles's self-serving *mot* is not endorsed. In its wry levity, however, this anecdote resembles one Defoe used on several occasions concerning 'Capt. Vratz, a Polander, who, in cold blood, assassinated an English gentleman ... and who, the day before he was to be hang'd for it, when he was spoken with by the minister to prepare himself for death, answer'd that *he did not doubt but God would have some respect to him as a gentleman*'.[31] In both cases, the tone of the story is less that of puritan indignation over a royal or genteel offender trying to exempt himself from divine rigour, than of grim amusement at such bizarre evasions.

In the Vratz anecdote and in Defoe's irony about the deity being too wellbred and genteel to punish misdeeds there is a note of class hostility. Other writers at the time similarly suggest that the Deists appeal to upper-class readers by freeing them from guilt or anxiety over their modish self-indulgences, and sparing their polite ears from unwelcome mention of hell. Thus Edward Young declares,

> Atheists are few; most nymphs a godhead own,
> And nothing but his *attributes* dethrone.
> From Atheists far, they stedfastly believe
> God is, and is almighty – to forgive.
> His other excellence they'll not dispute;
> But *mercy*, sure, is his chief attribute.
> Shall pleasures of a short duration chain
> A *lady's* soul in everlasting pain?
> Will the great author us poor worms destroy
> For now and then a sip of transient joy?
> No, he's for-ever in a smiling mood,
> He's like themselves; or how could he be good?
> And they blaspheme who blacker schemes suppose –
> Devoutly, thus, *Jehovah* they depose
> The *pure*! the *just*! and set up in his stead
> A Deity, that's perfectly *well bred*.[32]

A page earlier in the same poem (p. 21), Young alludes explicitly to Tindal: in church the 'well-drest *Belle*' who 'smiles to hear of hell' also 'casts an eye of sweet disdain on all, / Who listen less to *T—ll*, than St. *Paul*.' Alexander Pope's references to Tindal are more scathing, e.g.,

> But art thou one, whom new opinions sway,
> One, who believes as Tindal leads the way,
> Who Virtue and a Church alike disowns,
> Thinks that but words, and this but brick and stones?[33]

Pope asserts that the recently-deceased Tindal spurns ('disowns') both Virtue and Church, reducing the former to mere verbiage ('but words') and the latter to the establishments ('brick and stones') that house it. In view of the Deistic proclivities sometimes imputed to Pope himself, it is noteworthy that he represents Tindal as broaching shocking 'new opinions'. The second couplet is somewhat ambiguous: does Tindal cast off debate about morality or, more drastically and reprehensibly, morality itself? Does he repudiate clerical and ecclesiastical institutions or, more radically and perversely, religion itself? On either reading, Tindal is clearly being denounced as a false guide.[34]

The risk one takes in not believing is at the heart of the Pascalian wager, versions of which are broached in this book (as in the *Serious Reflections*) not once but twice. Toward the end of the penultimate chapter, defending the authenticity of Scripture, the author declares,

> suppose, *as we may well do*, that the Scripture should be the word of GOD, and that it is a real Revelation of his *Mind* and *Will*; what Condition will these Men ['disputing the veracity of the Scripture'] find themselves in then? and thus far is a certain Truth, and I think they will not dispute it, (*viz.*) that they are not sure of the Negative; nay, I will venture to go farther, the Affirmative is reasonable, the Negative only presumptive; that it is so, is probable; that it is not so is doubtful; and on which side lies the hazard? either there is no danger in the Negative, or these Men are unaccountably negligent of themselves, and strangely quiet and tranquil in the greatest imaginable Risque (see below, p. 49).

Near the end of the book, in the course of the '*APPENDIX; Affectionately address'd to the Youth of this Age, to prevent, if possible, their being early debauch'd with Atheistic and Deistic Principles*' (p. 57f. below), he returns to this argument. Having reasserted that Scripture 'is establish'd upon the Truth of that Being who is essential Truth it self, and is as surely his Word, as that there is a Heaven or an Earth, and as there is a Soul in Man', he continues,

> At least be pleas'd to look back to what has been said in this Work to prove it, and observe that you cannot be certain it is not so, and if the Affirmative should prove really true, how fatal will your Mistake be?
>
> *If it should so fall out, as who can tell,*
> *But there may be a* GOD, *a* HEAVEN, *and* HELL,
> *Mankind had best consider well, for Fear*
> *'T should be too late when their Mistakes appear* (p. 58 below).

'I would ask the most confident Atheist', Defoe says in the *Serious Reflections*,

> what Assurance he has of the Negative, and what a Risque he runs if he should be mistaken? This we are sure of, if we want [i.e. lack] Demonstration to prove the Being of a God, they are much more at a Loss for a Demonstration to prove the Negative. Now no Man can answer it to his Prudence, to take the Risque they run, upon an uncertain supposititious Notion ... Methinks these Gentlemen act with more Courage than

Discretion; for if it should happen at last, that there should be a God, and that he has the Power of Rewards and Punishments in his Hand, as he must have or cease to be Almighty, they are but in an ill Case.

Then follow the four verses just quoted.[35] Near the end of the same volume, in the appended 'VISION of the ANGELICK WORLD', Defoe tells the story of a university student who had fallen into atheism but is brought to renounce it: the catalyst to his dramatic conversion is reading aloud the same verses, with the final couplet altered from the third person to the more affecting 'Had I not best consider well, for fear / 'T shou'd be *too late*, when my Mistakes appear'.[36] To quote these four lines as a clinching argument in support of the Pascalian wager, one must have had hearty admiration for and good recall of Defoe's verse. In 1730 the heartiest admirer of Defoe's verse, and the writer most apt to remember and reproduce it in print, was undoubtedly Defoe himself. His fondness for quoting snatches of his own verse is a pattern I have traced elsewhere.[37]

If the divine origin and truth of Scripture were as incontestable as they are held to be in much of this book, the wager would be superfluous. Its inclusion is an implicit acknowledgement that the reader may *not* have been persuaded, and that there is room for doubt. By introducing the wager, the author stops trying to furnish substantive evidence for belief, and suggests instead that belief is more prudent than disbelief. The issue is no longer the relative validity of the theses themselves, but the practical consequences of embracing one or the other. What begins as an ontological question (does God exist or not?) turns into a pragmatic question (what are the benefits and dangers of affirming or denying his existence?). Instead of trying to prove that God exists, Defoe advocates through the wager merely that (having calculated the relative costs and benefits of our affirming or denying his existence) we prudently minimize our risk of grave loss by believing in him. Stated in these terms, Defoe's approach sounds less philosophical or theological than mercantile, as if he is recommending a promising and almost risk-free investment. Shaftesbury is predictably disdainful of this 'beggarly' way of thinking:

'Tis the most beggarly Refuge imaginable, which is so mightily cry'd up, and stands as a great Maxim with many able Men; 'that they shou'd strive to have *Faith*, and believe to the utmost: because if, after all, there be nothing in the matter, there will be no harm in being thus decev'd; but if there be any thing, it will be fatal for them not to have believ'd to the full'. But they are so far mistaken, that whilst they have this Thought, 'tis certain they can never believe either to their Satisfaction and Happiness in this World, or with any advantage of Recommendation to another. For besides that our Reason, which knows the Cheat, will never rest thorowly satisfy'd on such a Bottom, but turn us often a-drift, and toss us in a Sea of Doubt and Perplexity; we cannot but actually grow *worse* in our Religion, and entertain *a worse* Opinion still of *a Supreme* DEITY, whilst our Belief is founded on so injurious a Thought of him.[38]

Pascal's own use of the wager can be dignified through association with his mathematical background, in which working with unknowns and assessing probabilities were normal and appropriate mental habits. Defoe approached the wager from a somewhat different intellectual orientation, namely his involvement in questions of insurance, both theoretical and practical. As early as *An Essay upon Projects* (1697), he was a pioneering proponent of forms of social insurance, and at various points in his mercantile career he made or lost money by investing in, or purchasing coverage from, marine and fire insurance groups. Here the same principle is clearly at work. Prior to venturing upon a risky business like importing a cargo from Leghorn, or dying, it is prudent to take out an insurance policy. If your ship reaches port safely, or if it turns out that God does *not* exist, the insurance has cost little, and may have benefited you in other ways in the meantime. If your ship sinks, or if God *does* exist and calls you to a strict judgement, you have protected yourself against losing everything.

To compare belief in God with a purchase of insurance will strike some readers as bizarre or 'beggarly', and Defoe himself never makes the connection explicit. Yet as a way of confronting danger and uncertainty, this way of thinking was habitual to him, in mundane and lofty contexts alike. We do not know much about his private feelings and thoughts, but his published writings, and particularly the men and women who populate his novels, are much more preoccupied with anticipating, avoiding or minimizing disaster than with enjoying success. There is much more anxiety in the face of real or imagined threat than happiness in having escaped or triumphed over it.

We should also bear in mind that gambling was endemic to English culture in Defoe's day. Even though it was sometimes described in more euphemistic terms, betting was by no means confined to sports, games and races. When it went badly, as when the South Sea Bubble burst, gambling fever could be deplored or denounced on economic, social or moral grounds. Defoe joined the chorus of critics of the South Sea madness, and he was censorious about playing at cards or dice, yet gaming does not seem to have aroused in him any such indignation as he expressed about drinking, swearing and obscenity. Throughout the period there were many officially sanctioned institutions, such as lotteries, that catered for the gambling instinct. Even more pervasive and significant was the betting on events of the day. Whether (or when) an ailing queen might die, whether the British army or navy would be victorious

or vanquished in a given siege or battle, whether (or when) a merchant fleet
from the East Indies or the Mediterranean would arrive safely, whether the
harvest would be good or bad, which party would win an election: these and
countless other everyday uncertainties furnished constant matter for wagering. The events themselves obviously had great economic consequences – the
credit and prosperity of major trading companies and entire nations could
hinge on the results of a battle or a typhoon – but the wagering on such
eventualities could have significant social and economic impact as well. Then
as now, one could in effect bet on a rise or fall in the value of commodities
or shares in companies; then as now, one might try to take into account the
effect on such valuations of all pertinent contingencies, such as those just
mentioned. Defoe castigated the artificial, deceptive, conspiratorial manip-
ulation of share prices ('stock-jobbing'), and his comments on far-fetched
'projecting' schemes that he regarded as insubstantial, catchpenny speculations were similarly harsh. Yet he recognized that trade was subject to natural
and legitimate fluctuations in response to conditions that could change
suddenly and drastically, so that knowledge of what was happening in the
world was important to success in any market. In his periodical the *Review*
(1704–13), he insists on the crucial role of timely and accurate information
for sound planning and decision-making, whether by politicians, generals, or
tradesmen; although his *Review* deals more in editorializing than reporting,
he brings out repeatedly the malign effects of the party-inspired mistakes,
misjudgements and downright falsehoods that rival journalists impose on
their readers. In commerce the ability to buy, sell, invest or retrench profit-
ably depends partly on knowing the actual state of the market, and partly
on a weighing of likelihoods and contingencies without being able to anticipate fully what can or will happen. When the possibilities seem limited and
predictable, we call the process foresighted, judicious calculation; when the
uncertainties are greater, we tend to call it gambling. But 'dead certainty' is
rare if not impossible, and in its place are endless gradations of probability,
all of which entail more or less of a gamble.

In any case, the gambling mania was widespread at the time, versions
of it affected many areas of daily life, and some of Defoe's own commercial
undertakings early in his career seem to have been gambles in the most pejorative sense – excessively optimistic, risky and rash. Although bankruptcy
and other vicissitudes taught him a greater respect for prudence, if not more
actual prudence, he nevertheless continued throughout his life to value ven-
turesomeness as well, as the careers of his fictional heroes and heroines make
clear, and he treats risk-taking – virtually synonymous, after all, with betting,

gambling and wagering – as a valuable and in some circumstances necessary human trait. Thus to point out affinities between Defoe's wager concerning God's existence and a culture of insurance and gambling is neither to defend nor depreciate his way of thinking, but simply to suggest a relevant context for his adoption of this strategy in defence of religion. 'Relevant', of course, is a relative term, and some may deem it grotesque, if true, that Defoe could have had such prosaic, worldly doings in mind when he presumed to argue in God's behalf. But in treating religious matters, Defoe was scarcely inhibited by scruples about mixing the profane with the sacred. On the contrary, this is a recurrent and striking feature of his handling of Biblical characters, events and texts.

Revelation *versus* Reason

According to this book, things have always happened exactly as they had been foretold in the Bible: the unerring, chronologically exact fulfilment of prophecy confirms the veracity of Scripture, and validates its divine authorship. Scripture itself is used as evidence for the soundness of Scriptural prophecies, which in turn are used as the chief support for Scripture being God's word. The circularity of this reasoning characterizes much of the book: theses supposedly being tested and proved – e.g., that Scripture is a faithful expression of the divine will, and an accurate record of God's dealings with man – are treated as established, incontrovertible facts.

Such forecasts, borne out by actual happenings, are held to be beyond human power, and beyond the devil's power as well:

> let them tell us, what human Prescience could foretel things so remote in Time, so particular in Circumstance, as the Scripture does, and which have so critically been fulfill'd; let them give the least rational Account of any other Power, from Earth or Hell, that could do this ... If this can be done by the hand of Man, or by any human Art, I would gladly hear some Examples of the kind, and some intimation of any Person who ever pretended to it: Even the Devil, whose Power of Prediction, some have suggested to be great, tho' Reason dictates, that there is nothing of that kind in his Power, could not reach to these wonderful things, nor to any thing like them (pp. 49, 47 below).

Whether Satan can foresee or predict future events is immaterial to the present argument; Deists had questioned the prophecies in the Old Testament, but had not claimed that they were the devil's doing. Yet this is a recurrent issue in the writings of Defoe, who insists that prescience belongs to God alone, and that all other pretences to it, satanic or human, are fraudulent.[39]

As a corollary, this book advances the view that errors would have been bound to creep into the text if its authors were mere human beings: 'If it were the word of a Man, the Failings and Imperfections of human Nature, would some where or other appear ... it would bewray its Author by its Imperfections, and might, for that Reason [alone], be doubted' (see p. 46 below). But because it has no such blemishes – 'its whole Tenour is like its Author, one body of universal Truth' – it is beyond what even the best of men could have produced, and must be God's word. Problematic Biblical passages were to be accounted for increasingly, in the course of the Eighteenth Century, as the handiwork of fallible human authors. But this author treats questions of translation, transmission and so on as quibbles over non-essentials. The 'gainsayers of the Age' raise 'innumerable Cavils at the Letter of it, the Diction, the Manner, the Translations, the Difficulties in the Reading, the Inconsistencies, which they call irreconcilable, and the like'; they find 'some Difficulties in the reading, seeming Contradictions, wrong Translations, Errors in the Copies, and the like,' but they refuse to acknowledge 'that which is plain, congruous, undeniable, and against which no such Objection lies'.[40]

The Deists regard man as naturally reasonable, and reason as adequate to his needs; to them, revelation is at best superfluous and dispensable, at worst a heap of priestly fraud and imposition. The present author seeks to vindicate the authenticity and the necessity of revelation, and to challenge the alleged power of reason and human self-sufficiency.[41] One way to lessen the prestige of reason is to quote a line from Rochester's *Satyre Against Reason and Mankind*: '*Reason which fifty times for one does err*' (see p. 10 and explanatory note 23 below). For someone intent on defending orthodox Christianity against Deists, freethinkers and atheists, to quote Rochester is a startling strategy – or rather, it would be if the author were (as most respondents to Tindal seem to have been) a Church of England or Nonconformist cleric. To bring in Rochester as a reputable witness, as is done here, is entirely characteristic of Defoe, however, for whom there was no occasion too sacred for an apt verse of Rochester, and no occasion too profane for an apt verse of Scripture.[42] Such a citation would have been unthinkable for most divines, who could see little merit in Rochester's life or works, apart from his deathbed repentance.[43] Yet the present author endorses Rochester's view that the inadequacy of reason is shown by its proneness to error, and particularly by the blunders that even the wisest men have made on the subjects of thinking, knowing, and reason itself.[44]

Early in the first chapter he tells us,

God having created the Carcase of a Man, for 'tis evident the Body was first form'd, breath'd into him the *Breath of Life*: There was Nature entirely form'd; he receiv'd Life from God; but it does not appear that this Natural Life had any Religious Powers till afterward, when Man became also *a living Soul*, which it is evident was subsequent to his Natural Powers.

Natural Power, which is no more than the sensitive Life, the Locomotive, and other Faculties in common with Brutes, could have no discovery of God, as we see demonstrated too often in the demented Carcase of a Man born an Idiot, inanimate or deprived of the Use of his Reason, which is the Soul; whether by any organnick Impotence, or other occult Defect which Philosophy cannot account for.

Nature then has no Religious Powers, and to say *Natural Religion* is indeed to say nothing, or nothing to the Purpose; 'tis in short to talk Nonsense, a Jargon of Words without Meaning, like the Man of Nature himself without a Soul (pp. 6–7 below).

At this point reason is identified with the soul, not denigrated, yet it is treated as neither an original feature of the human constitution nor an inseparable, indispensable human property. By introducing comparisons with 'Brutes', 'a Man born an Idiot', and 'the Man of Nature', the present author alludes to factors that had seemed relevant, at least since Descartes, to the philosophical task of defining and distinguishing the human. Defoe considered them at some length in a work about the 'wild boy' who had been brought to England from Hanover, entitled *Mere Nature Delineated: or, a Body without a Soul* (1726).[45] These were topics of widespread current interest, yet it seems noteworthy that both Defoe's work and the present passage use 'inanimate' rather peculiarly (that is, to mean 'soulless', a sense not recorded by the *OED*); both entertain the possibility of a human body 'without a Soul'; and more generally, both take a dim view of 'mere' nature, rather than aggrandizing it as do the Deists.

Denying that Adam was fully in possession of reason from the moment of his creation, the author observes here that according to Genesis, man's body was created before his soul, spirit, or reason; these were put into man by God, who withheld them from the rest of created nature. Adam existed before God gave him spirit, soul or reason, just as animals (and, it would seem, idiots) continue to exist without them. If God endowed Adam only in stages, then his way of making man was of a piece with the gradual process by which he revealed his will to man. Although it does not lessen the value of reason itself, this point is helpful to the critique of Tindal, who holds that everything essential was there from the very beginning, *'as Old as the Creation'*. Possession of reason, spirit and soul links man to God and differentiates him from the rest of created nature. For the critic of Deism, however, the crucial factor is not that these attributes are God-*like* but that they are God-*given*: they do not raise man to God's level, but (as with successive revelations) they enable man to understand God's will toward him. Although reason was adequate to Adam's needs before the fall, it was not perfect even then, because that would have made Adam equal to God, and thus a god himself. By aggrandizing the strength of human reason, and its role in governing our thoughts and actions, the Deists elevate mankind to godlike status, and thus recapitulate Satan's way of deluding Eve. To be equal with God is to *be* God: in the words of the text, 'If Reason is perfectly enlightned, if it has a self-sufficiency of Knowledge; in a word, if it is infinite in Prescience, and incapable of farther Information, then Reason is GOD; for whatsoever is Infinite is Eternal, *and that is God*... Reason is erected, as before, into an Equality with Infinite, and is set up for a God' (p. 9 below). Defoe tends to be unusually truculent on the subject of idolatry. In China and Mongolia in the *Farther Adventures*, the spectacle of benighted people paying obeisance to grotesque artifacts that they themselves have created kindles in Crusoe an anger and loathing that Defoe evidently regards as justified. Indeed, God himself is regularly incensed on similar grounds in the Old Testament, and responds vehemently: among 'the reasons annexed to the second commandment, the more to enforce it', are God's 'fervent zeal for his own worship, and his revengeful indignation against all false worship ... accounting the breakers of this commandment such as hate him' (*The Larger Catechism*, A. 110). In the present work, the Deists are accused of aggrandizing human reason to a parity with God's, and thus making man an object of idolatrous worship.

Another objection is that human reason was drastically impaired by the fall. Instead of punishing Adam and Eve for their transgression by striking them dead, God relented and again assisted man, not by restoring his reason to its full strength, but by supplementing man's stock of knowledge through further revelations. Revelation has been an ongoing, incremental process, which reached a climax with the promulgation of the Gospel by Jesus and his disciples. After the apostolic age, stunning disclosures authenticated by miracles were no longer called for, because the Scriptural text, the church and the ministry were all in place.

The inadequacy of reason is shown further by its very struggles to improve and extend itself, and by man's constant efforts to learn more. Thus a personified reason is said to confess her own limitations 'by her constant assiduous Endeavours and unwearied Application after farther Illumination: *Reason* directs us openly to an incessant Search after Knowledge; this I must take for a certain sign that she is sensible of her present Defficiency' (p. 9). Either through sleight of hand or confusion, the author treats knowledge and reason as the same thing, in order to downgrade reason. Seeking to enlarge our knowledge does not, of course, necessarily impugn our mental endowments. This fallacious argument is one that Defoe uses, however, in writings concerned with perplexing natural phenomena, largely to magnify God's power over them, but also to lessen the prestige of reason. For the purposes of Tindal and other Deists, it is not necessary for reason to be perfect or infallible (although that assumption is imputed to them in the present book); ordinarily they contend merely that reason is the best and (together with experience) the only tool we have to obtain or test our knowledge. On this view, anything purporting to be a divine revelation, now or in the remote past, must be accepted or rejected in the light of reason and experience. But this is to accord reason a higher authority than revelation, and thus to overturn the proper hierarchy, as the author sees it.

Breakdowns of proper order become, in fact, objects of alarm and indignation in a number of Defoe's later writings: not only violations of '*The Great Law of Subordination*' in the family and society, but also those affecting religious and metaphysical hierarchies. Thus he deplores the elevation of reason over revelation partly as a challenge to God's paramount role in the universe, and partly as a shocking presumption, as if reason and its apologists are the same kind of order-inverting upstarts as chambermaids who dress more modishly and give themselves more airs than their mistresses. Defoe's task is to reassert the just rule of God and the heads of households in their respective realms, as well as to satirize those seeking to deny and usurp their authority. The present book addresses a similar challenge, and affirms similarly conservative principles.

Reason is a powerful, complex, and usually positive word for early eighteenth-century authors, but Defoe's use of it varies. In *Jure Divino*, where he attacks the theory that kings rule by divine right, he invokes reason against what he sees as pseudo-historical mystification: sound principles of governance are associated with reason, and contrasted with fanciful myths and customs contrived to justify royal absolutism. Against non-jurors, high-flying Tories and other Stuart apologists and Jacobite sympathizers, Defoe's method and tone resemble those of the Deists, who challenge priestly obfuscation, superstition and fraud in the name of reason. But on religious questions, his assumptions and procedures are quite different; he emphasizes the limitations of reason, and consistently subordinates it to revelation, as is done in the present work.

For Defoe, the principle that reason must defer or give way to revelation applies not only to religious issues, but to unresolved 'scientific' problems as well. This is most striking in his discussion of winds in *The Storm* (1704) and of plagues in *A Journal of the Plague Year* (1722). In each case, he records competing hypotheses about the nature and source of a phenomenon, but finds none of them adequate. If he had been a thorough-going Modern, fully sharing the assumptions and ambitions of his Royal Society contemporaries, he would have concluded that further observation and experimentation was necessary, that the seeming mysteries would eventually be solved, and that hurricanes and plagues would turn out to obey natural laws. But Defoe does not take this step. Instead, he declares that God has hidden some things from our understanding, with the intention of forcing us to acknowledge his providential interventions in the created universe, as well as our own limitations – i.e. that reason has reached the end of its tether, beyond which we must rely on revelation.[46] According to Defoe, if we give up the search for rational explanations too soon, our piety may be commendable but we are in some danger of superstition: 'I know some are apt to entitle the Hand of God, to the common and most ridiculous Trifles in nature; as a religious Creature, I knew, seeing a Bottle of Beer being over ripe burst out, the Cork fly up against the Ceiling, and the Froth follow it like an Engin, cried out, *O! the Wonders of Omnipotent Power*'.[47] Defoe can thus distance himself from the 'Extremes these Things may lead weak People into', but the opposite extreme he sees as more dangerous: if we refuse to recognize any bounds to our scientific knowledge and insist on pressing forward, we not only exhibit an exaggerated confidence in human reason, but by implicitly denying God's role in the matter, we are on the verge of atheism. Meteorology and epidemiology have since cleared up many of the phenomena that puzzled Defoe, but my point is not that he gave up (or advocated giving up) the attempt to understand them too readily. Rather, it is that for a quarter of a century, he had consistently upheld revelation as a source of truth before which mere reason must bow. This traditional position was under overt attack at the time by Deists, but it is maintained insistently in the present work.

Defoe's affirmation of revelation in works like the *Serious Reflections* and *A New Family Instructor* takes two main forms, each of which has various ramifications. One is to defend the *necessity* of revelation, against the Deistic contention that reason, building on experience, is all that mankind really has or needs. The other is to defend the *fact* of revelation, both in the sense that God has chosen to vouchsafe to mankind direct communications of his actions and intentions, and in the sense that Scripture contains a full and accurate record of these actions and intentions, written at God's inspiration or dictation. These represent the positive side of his case, in the course of which he affirms various beliefs which he regards as either contributing to or following from the credibility of revelation: for instance, that nearly all the scriptural prophecies have been fulfilled, and the rest will be in due course; that God has not only revealed *that* he is to be worshipped, but specified *how*; that Jesus was the promised Messiah, and that salvation is possible only through faith in him.

But Defoe's responses to Deism are seldom confined to upholding Christian doctrine – which is just as well, since these defences are often no more than assertions of credal points backed by proof-texts from Scripture, the authority of which is exactly what the Deists are contesting. Equally prominent, and on the whole more effective, are Defoe's attacks on the assumptions that he sees underlying the Deists' own positions, and on the consequences that he thinks follow from them. *Christianity Not as Old as the Creation* concentrates on exposing weaknesses in the Deists' case, a polemical strategy characteristic of the Deists as well, who devote greater energy and ingenuity to exposing flaws in the Bible, and in the religious institutions based upon it, than to expounding a superior theology of their own. Indeed, the absence of any agreed-upon body of positive doctrine tends to support the contention of some modern historians that Deism does not really represent a coherent movement. Although the persons traditionally identified as Deists share various objections to revelation and priestcraft, and various rhetorical methods for attacking them, they were probably more closely associated in the minds of their opponents than among themselves, and in this sense they fall short of the collaborative (not to say conspiratorial) community that we tend to think of as forming a 'movement'.[48]

Another line of orthodox response to the Deists' aggrandizement of reason was historical: that is, a contention that although the complete, culminating expression of divine will did not occur until the promulgation of the gospel, this era had been preceded by a process of revelation that was gradual and incremental, recorded throughout the Old Testament, and in any case going well beyond what had been communicated to Adam when he was created (or after he fell). Those asserting the necessity of revelation and denying the sufficiency of reason sometimes joined historical with anthropological arguments: they maintained that the evidence from pagan antiquity, like that from modern Africa, Asia and the Americas, points to drastically varying stages of civilization, and that these cannot be accounted for by man's natural, rational endowments, which should make for greater uniformity. Instead, critics of the adequacy and strength of reason explained the great worldwide variation in man's mental attainments either in terms of the differing degrees of enlightenment that God has vouchsafed to mankind in different times and places, or (from a seemingly opposed but often shared perspective) in terms of the differing degrees of degeneration various races have undergone since the Fall. According to Defoe, Christian believers had a monopoly on 'saving truth', on knowing what was necessary for salvation.[49] And thanks to their (relative) freedom from the communal errors and falsehoods that darken and disable most human minds, they enjoyed advantageous (but by no means exclusive) access to truth itself.

From a modern perspective, both the historical and the anthropological evidence worked in the Deists' favour. The actual *findings* of both kinds of research tended to undermine Christianity: for example, by associating it with the religions of many other times and places that claim to be based on direct, exclusive divine revelation. Historical and anthropological *methods* were also damaging to traditional Christian belief: as new tools of philological and comparative critical analysis were brought to bear on the Biblical text, the unitary, authoritative divine word increasingly came to be seen as a rather miscellaneous collection of very human documents.

Original Sin, Guilt, Fear and Folly

The conception of Christianity in this book contains a strong element of anxiety. That God should be feared as well as loved is a prominent theme in the Old Testament, in which his chosen people repeatedly provoke his angry, punitive side, and suffer the drastic consequences. When they challenge God directly by violating the first four commandments they ignite his fury, but they also inflame him when they transgress any of the other six. They are repeatedly subjected to divine punishment, whether administered directly from on high, or by means of human agents like the Babylonians. They fall into sin time after time; no single cause is identified for their doing so, yet the pattern is so constant that the notion of original sin might well seem a plausible inference from it, even if there were no such 'historical' source as the story of Adam and Eve in Genesis. The Old Testament is thus an endless chronicle of crime and punishment – of man's infractions kindling God's wrath and dreadful retribution, both of which give rise to human shame, guilt and fear.

The Deists find nearly every ingredient in this recipe (and nearly every stage in this causal sequence) unnatural, and therefore incredible and repugnant on moral, psychological and historical grounds alike. The Deists think God must be supremely and impeccably reasonable, but in the Old Testament he seems to them so petty, vindictive, hot-tempered and generally irrational as to be pathologically human rather than godlike. The amount of soothing, placating, flattering obeisance his jealousy and wrath require proves (to the Deists) that such a god must be a human contrivance, the handiwork of priestcraft. Priests pretend that they alone can avert or lessen earthquakes, floods, famines, pestilence and the other vindictive gestures of such a god. Priests alone, the Deists believe, are capable of making up such a god, and such appalling stories about him, so as to frighten weak and ignorant people into paying them to keep this angry god of theirs at bay. By rejecting the doctrine of original sin, the Deists take a step away from Christianity. If human nature is and has always been free from any such blemish, and man has never transgressed against his obligations to a supremely reasonable God, then there is no need for reconciliation with an offended deity through sacrifice, expiation, imputed righteousness, or any of the other mediatorial functions served, in orthodox Christianity, by Jesus Christ. His mission to save mankind need not be denied explicitly by the Deists, since they have rendered any such mission superfluous: mankind has committed no sin or crime that requires divine forgiveness (nor is there any hell to save mankind *from*).

Christianity cannot be as old as creation, the present author contends, because there was no occasion for it as long as Adam and Eve remained in their unfallen state. He argues that some time had to elapse between Adam's creation, his fall, and the promulgation to him of the doctrine of sacrificial redemption, on which Christianity rests: if a passage of time is acknowledged, then Christianity cannot be as old as creation. Christ the son must indeed be coeternal with God the father, but his mission of redeeming mankind from sin, which is the basis of Christianity, begins only after sin has come into the world, with God's sentence on the serpent that 'I will put enmity between thee and the woman, and between thy seed and her seed: and it shall bruise thy head, and thou shalt bruise his heel' (Genesis 3:15, as quoted on p. 31 below). This argument takes for granted, of course, that Genesis is an accurate record of early dealings between God and man. Instead of confining himself to the Biblical version of this historical sequence, however, the present author extrapolates from its few details a story very reminiscent of Defoe's writings: specifically, of passages discussing the psychological association between guilt and fear, dramatizing the tribulations of anxious sinners as criminal trials, and characterizing Adam as a fool. None of these is required by (or contributes to) a refutation of Tindal, yet all are recurrent Defoean *topoi*.

That guilt is a *source* of fear is a commonplace, but one that Defoe never tired of reiterating.[50] The related notion that fear is a symptom or manifestation of guilt is distinctly (though not uniquely) Defoean; instead of being a *pro*spective emotion, as it is usually considered, fear becomes essentially *ret-*

*ro*spective, a sign of past misdeeds. Thus the unexceptionable contention that if you're guilty you're liable to be fearful turns into a more arguable one, that if you're fearful, it's *because* you're guilty (or that if you weren't guilty, you wouldn't be fearful). Whatever the psychological or moral soundness of this thesis, Defoe's commitment to it, and his interest in illustrating its often grim or grotesque effects on human behaviour, may be the best explanation of the attention paid here, at pp. 39–40 below, to Adam and Eve's guilt-bespeaking fright.

The further implication, that guilt produces not only fear but folly, is also drawn elsewhere in Defoe's writings, which suggest that Adam behaved foolishly, partly as a consequence of his guilt and fear, and partly because his transgression had reduced him to a mere fool. Folly came into the world (as did guilt) through the fall: Adam's drastically impaired intellect made him a fit object of satire,[51] even though filial loyalty prevented most writers before Defoe from lampooning him. I know of no other writer so contemptuous of his own hapless ancestor.[52] In this respect, however, the present author is at one with Defoe, who regards Adam and Eve as ordinary human beings like himself, and insists on the fallibility and frailty of various Biblical figures, such as the disciples in their weaker moments.[53] Here the remarks on Adam's actions after the fall (p. 40 below) are the liveliest part of the book, because discussion of theological abstractions gives way to a moment of narrative. Compared with Defoe's brash updating of Genesis and *Paradise Lost* in the *Political History of the Devil*, this passage does not fully exploit its dramatic potential. Yet it similarly interprets and expands, at once shrewdly and satirically, the laconic text of Genesis, and similarly assigns understandable (if discreditable) motives to actions sketchily summarized in the Bible. Its brusque impatience with the guilty Adam, and its emphasis on the absurdity rather than the pathos of his weak shuffling, are very characteristic of Defoe. The presentation of Adam as if on trial in court provides another suggestive affinity, both substantive and stylistic, to Defoe's known works.[54]

The ninth of the Articles of Religion in *The Book of Common Prayer*, 'Of Original or Birth-Sin', begins,

Original Sin ... is the fault and corruption of the Nature of every man, that naturally is ingendered of the offspring of Adam; whereby man is very far gone from original righteousness, and is of his own nature inclined to evil, so that the flesh lusteth always contrary to the spirit; and therefore in every person born into this world, it deserveth God's wrath and damnation.

The corresponding passage in the *Westminster Confession*, *'Of the Fall of Man, of Sin, and of the Punishment thereof*, amplifies the same doctrine with Calvinist rigour. Its first four paragraphs declare,

> OUR first parents being seduced by the subtilty and temptation of Satan, sinned in eating the forbidden fruit. This their sin God was pleased, according to his wise and holy counsel, to permit, having purposed to order it to his own glory. ¶ By this sin they fell from their original righteousness, and communion with God, and so became dead in sin, and wholly defiled in all the faculties and parts of soul and body. ¶ They being the root of all mankind, the guilt of this sin was imputed, and the same death in sin and corrupted nature conveyed to all their posterity, descending from them by ordinary generation. ¶ From this original corruption, whereby we are utterly indisposed, disabled, and made opposite to all good, and wholly inclined to all evil, do proceed all actual transgressions.

This is the orthodox image of the fall of man, and the subsequent plight of humanity. Tindal regards it as 'a Libel on the Dignity of human Nature; and an high Reflection on the Wisdom and Goodness of its Author; in placing them, without any Fault of theirs, in an unavoidable State of Degeneracy and Corruption for 4,000 Years together, and continuing the greatest Part still in the same State'.[55] Tindal also pretends to be perplexed by various details in the Biblical account of the Fall: he cannot understand 'how *Eve* cou'd entertain a Conference with a Serpent (incapable of human Voice) even before Consent had giv'n any Meaning to Sounds'; he wonders why Adam and Eve, 'tho' they knew not what Cloaths were, [should] be asham'd to be seen uncloath'd by one another, and by God himself'; and he is puzzled by 'their *Fig-leave Aprons*, which *they*, (having, it seems, all Things necessary for sewing) *sew'd together*'.[56] The point of his drollery is that the Genesis narrative, ridiculous in itself, cannot provide a credible foundation for the Christian doctrines of original sin or innate depravity; and more generally, that here and elsewhere the Old Testament portrait of God is so grotesque and sinister as to discredit the Christian belief in it as divine revelation.

On this subject, Defoe's position was consistent throughout his career. Four decades earlier he had written, 'So swift are Men to desperate Ills design'd, / To ill spontaneous, and in good confin'd. A proof the evil Principle is first, / And Guilt has all the Power to Will engross'd'.[57] In 'A Vision of the Angelick World', he declared that 'our Propensity to Evil rather than Good, is a Testimony of the original Depravity of human Nature'.[58] In the *Family Instructor I*, a father explains to his child that 'the Effect of that First Man's Sin is a corrupt Taint which we all bring into the World with us, and which we find upon our Nature, by which we find a Natural Propensity in us to do Evil, and no Natural Inclination to do Good'.[59]

In the present work, the Deists' denial of the doctrine of original sin provokes the author to a resolute restatement of Calvinist orthodoxy. Sin is said to be 'in the very Man as a Creature, twisted with his very Soul[;] his very Reason, which is pretended to be his Infallible Guide, is corrupted and debauch'd ... it is not only in some, but in all; it is not this or that Man, or a few Men that are wicked, but, in short, Mankind are tainted; the whole Race is touch'd with the Infirmity; Death passed upon all Men; for that all have sinned' (p. 41 below). 'This general Depravity' is treated as a fact, founded on the account in Genesis, yet confirmed by our common experience as well as by history. By challenging it, the Deists are at a loss to find out

> an Original for Crime; and especially for the Universality of Crime; and above all, for its being, as above, gotten into the very Soul of the Creature, mixt with his Understanding, and possest of all his reasoning Powers, and Faculties. How comes the original Propensity to offend, and whence is it prevalent, even against the opposition, which in some Cases Reason makes against it? I leave them to reply to these things at leisure. (p. 42 below)

To allege an 'original Propensity to offend', 'powerful Inclinations to do Evil', a 'Propensity to Evil rather than Good' and the like, as these latter-day defences of orthodoxy do, moderates the tone but not the substance of a vision of mankind 'wholly defiled in all the faculties and parts of soul and body', and 'utterly indisposed, disabled, and made opposite to all good, and wholly inclined to all evil'. Defoe's versions are not as unqualified or truculent as those of the *Westminster Confession of Faith*, but they retain its emphasis on man's incapacity to attain salvation through his own merits. In any case, the differences between the divines assembled at Westminster around 1640 and Defoe writing eighty or ninety years later seem minor, compared with the vast gulf on this subject between him and his Deist contemporaries in the 1720s.

The author of *Christianity Not as Old as the Creation* is an adherent to Protestant orthodoxy. By citing here and in the explanatory notes the *Book of Common Prayer* and the *Westminster Confession of Faith* alike, I have tried to indicate that on doctrinal questions there is no real difference between them. This is to say, as Defoe himself said on various occasions, that whatever disagreements there may have been between the Church of England and Dissent about proper church organization, liturgy and ritual, they were in full agreement on substantive matters of belief.[60] But even though the two communities shared officially the same articles of faith, both had by the Eighteenth Century chosen to downplay or disregard some of the more harshly Calvinistic ones, without explicitly repudiating them. The most glaring instance was the doctrine of God's eternal decrees of election and reprobation ('By the decree of God, for the manifestation of his glory, some men and angels are predestinated unto everlasting life, and others foreordained to everlasting death': see *Westminster Confession of Faith*, ch. 3, ¶ 3). The idea of predestination evokes the Deists' keenest scorn, although they pretend that it is heathen or hypothetical gods they are mocking. This particular doctrine is not upheld in the present work;[61] for the most part, however, *Christianity Not as Old as the Creation*, like Defoe's hitherto known writings, does defend Calvinist positions against what are represented as mistaken or malicious Deistic deviations. This is to suggest that on theological questions, Defoe was conservative rather than progressive. To some readers this will seem surprising in itself, out of keeping with an image of him as in the intellectual vanguard, a forward-looking '*Citizen of the Modern World*.'[62] But Defoe's religious thinking, without simply recapitulating that of Calvin – who had written, after all, nearly two centuries earlier – is very much within the Calvinist tradition. At all events, the Reformation had begun in a spirit of recovery and reaffirmation, and in Defoe's writings on religion during the last decade of his life, there is a similar suggestion that the world has gone astray, and is to be restored not through theological innovation, particularly of the Deistic variety, but by reviving a still-available, still-retrievable past.

This work nevertheless softens some of the asperities of the *Westminster Confession of Faith*, and occasionally deviates from the substance as well as the tone of 'pure' Calvinism. For example, *Christianity Not as Old as the Creation* implies that whether to believe or not is within one's choice. The Pascalian wager depends on weighing alternatives and reaching a deliberate decision, and much of the book, most notably the '*APPENDIX; Affectionately address'd to the Youth of this Age, to prevent, if possible, their being early debauch'd with Atheistic and Deistic Principles*', similarly implies that faith is in our control, something that we can venture upon or reject as we wish. Yet according to Calvin, it is vain to suppose that faith is a matter of active human volition; an all-powerful God confers or withholds it as he pleases, so that the individual must be essentially passive and dependent on the divine will. On this crucial issue, the *Westminster Confession of Faith* remains firmly Calvinist, but *Christianity Not as Old as the Creation* does not.

Why God doesn't Destroy the Devil, and Other Fridayesque Questions

In *Christianity Not as Old as the Creation*, the 'innumerable Cavils and Scruples' (p. 80 below) raised by the Deists about the inspired status of Scripture, and about the dealings between God and man set forth in it, are treated as too contrived or insubstantial to merit detailed refutation. Yet despite its occasionally peremptory manner, this work recognizes that some of the Deists' contentions cannot be dismissed out of hand. Throughout his writings of the preceding decade, Defoe had shown an awareness of the difficulties posed by the Deists; although they finally seem not to have shaken his belief, they evidently worried him, and far from reducing his opponents to men of straw, he sometimes stated their positions quite forcefully. The best illustrations of this pattern occur in *Robinson Crusoe* and the *Serious Reflections*. Both precede Tindal's *Christianity as Old as the Creation*, of course, but I will juxtapose them with that book, partly to indicate that Defoe was justified in treating the Deists as sharing arguments in a common cause, and partly to suggest that he was able to respond to Tindal's book with extraordinary rapidity because he had already been wrestling with some of its leading topics for more than a decade.

On the question of why God continues to allow Satan to 'range about deceiving, and circumventing Mankind', Tindal observes,

> THE poor *Indians* ... when our Missionaries give such an Account of the Devil, say, 'is not your God a good God, and loves Mankind? Why does he then permit this Devil to be continually doing them such infinite Hurt? Why is he not put under Confinement, if not depriv'd of a Being, of which he has made himself unworthy? With us One, who does not hinder a Mischief, when it is in his Power, is thought not much better than he who does it.'[63]

I have not attempted to trace Tindal's source among the many accounts by Spanish, French or English missionaries of their dealings with American natives. He may have drawn on the writings of actual missionaries, such as those published by the Jesuits in their famous series of *Lettres édifiantes et curieuses* from various parts of the world. But he might also have had in mind the dialogue on the subject between Robinson Crusoe and Friday (in *Novels*, vol. 1, pp. 218–19). When Crusoe 'had been telling him how the Devil was God's Enemy in the Hearts of Men, and used all his Malice and Skill to defeat the good Designs of Providence, and to ruine the Kingdom of Christ in the World; and the like', Friday inquires, '*if God much strong, much might as the Devil, why God no kill the Devil, so make him no more do wicked?*' Crusoe is nonplussed by this question, but comes up with the answer that '*God will at last punish him severely*; he is *reserv'd for the Judgment, and is to be cast into the Bottomless-Pit, to dwell with everlasting Fire*'. But '*This did not satisfie Friday*', who says, '*RESERVE, AT LAST, me no understand; but, Why not kill the Devil now, not kill great ago?*' Crusoe unwarily responds, '*You may as well ask me, said I, Why God does not kill you and I, when we do wicked Things here that* offend him? We are preserv'd to repent and be pardon'd'. At this point Friday springs a Deistic mousetrap: 'He muses a while at this; *well, well,* says he, mighty affectionately, *that well; so you, I Devil, all wicked, all preserve, repent, God pardon all*. 'Here I was run down again by him to the last Degree', Crusoe confesses, nor does he try to reason Friday out of his heretical supposition that Satan, along with all human sinners, will ultimately be saved. Instead, he falls back on Scripture, and the rest of the paragraph is worth quoting in full, because it expresses a conviction articulated at greater length in *Christianity Not as Old as the Creation*. Friday's unorthodox belief in universal salvation, Crusoe declares,

> was a Testimony to me, how the meer Notions of Nature, though they will guide reasonable Creatures to the Knowledge of a God, and of a Worship or Homage due to the supreme Being of God, as a Consequence of our Nature; yet nothing but divine Revelation can form the Knowledge of *Jesus Christ*, and of a Redemption purchas'd for us, of a Mediator of the new Covenant, and of an Intercessor, at the Foot-stool of God's Throne; I say, nothing but a Revelation from Heaven, can form these in the Soul, and that therefore the Gospel of our Lord and Saviour *Jesus Christ*; I mean, the Word of God, and the Spirit of God promis'd for the Guide and Sanctifier of his People, are the absolutely necessary Instructors of the Souls of Men, in the saving Knowledge of God, and the Means of Salvation.

If God does not prevent the Devil's mischief, even though it is in his power to do so, then (Tindal and the 'poor *Indians*' infer) he cannot be much better than the Devil; he is either too weak to control Satan's malice, or he is complicit in it. The Deists seek to avoid this dilemma, posed as they see it by the Christian conception of God, by postulating an altogether benign God who will see to it that one and all are eventually redeemed, and by diminishing the role of the Devil (as of Providence) in their cosmology. From an orthodox standpoint, the Deists' strategy does not resolve the problem of evil, but merely denies or trivializes it. Tindal introduces the Fridayesque perplexity over Satan to make the same point that he reiterates elsewhere in *Christianity as Old as the Creation*, namely that the Biblical account of God's dealings with mankind impugns both his omnipotence and his benevolence. Defoe introduces it with a very different objective, but it is remarkable that he raises the issue at all, especially since Crusoe, far from being given arguments that might dispel Friday's doctrinally unsound hypotheses, is forced to acknowledge that he is 'run down ... by him to the last Degree'. But instead of capitulating to Friday's Deistic logic, Crusoe is able to reduce Friday's reasoning to 'the meer Notions of Nature', which can carry one only so far: that is, to a knowledge that God exists, and that some sort of 'Worship or Homage' is 'due to the supreme Being'. At this point, in Defoe's view, reason must give way to faith. The next stage of religious knowledge, 'absolutely necessary' for salvation, depends on 'divine Revelation', 'the Word of God' contained in the Gospels. Without it, the Deists' pretensions to 'natural religion' or a 'religion of nature' are of no avail. With it, Crusoe and Friday have 'the *sure Guide* to Heaven', and enjoy 'comfortable Views of the Spirit of God teaching and instructing us by his Word, *leading us into all Truth*' – which (Defoe believes) they could not have reached through experience and reason alone.[64]

Equally striking in its way is a passage in the *Serious Reflections*, in which Crusoe observes how small a fraction of mankind is Christian, for 'in all the Voyages and Travels which I have employ'd two Volumes in giving a Relation of, I never set my Foot in a Christian Country, no not in circling three Parts of the Globe'. His comment is worth quoting at length:

> It is ... a melancholy Reflection to think, how all these Parts of the World, and with infinite Numbers of Millions of People, furnish'd with the Powers of Reason, and Gifts of Nature, and many Ways, if not every Way, as capable of the Reception of sublime things, as we are, are yet abandon'd to the grossest Ignorance and Depravity ... What the Divine Wisdom has determined concerning the Souls of so many Millions, it is hard to conclude ... If they are received to Mercy in a Future State, according to the Opinion of some, as having not sin'd against saving Light, then their Ignorance and Pagan Darkness is not a Curse, but a Felicity; and there are no unhappy People in the World, but those lost among Christians, for their Sins against reveal'd Light; nay, then being born in the Regions of Christian Light, and under the Revelation of the Gospel Doctrines, is not so much as Mercy to be acknowledged as some teach us, and it may in a negative Manner be true, that the Christian Religion is an Efficient in the Condemnation of Sinners, and loses more than it saves, which is impious but to imagin: On the other Hand, if all those Nations are concluded under the Sentence of eternal Absence from God, which is Hell in the Abstract; then what becomes of all the sceptical Doctrines of its being inconsistent with the Mercy and Goodness of an infinite and beneficent Being, to condemn so great a Part of the World, for not believing in him of whom they never had any Knowledge or Instruction?[65]

Decades earlier, in the *Review*, Defoe had denied that a Turk can be saved, and justified his view (in response to a reader's objection) by citing the Biblical affirmation,

> that *whoever believes i.e.* in the Lord Jesus Christ, *shall be sav'd*; and *whoever believes not, shall be Damned*. That if Christ be not in us *reprobati sumus*, that is, Out-Casts; that *there is no other Name under Heaven, by which a Man can be sav'd*; and a Multitude of other Places in Scripture, which limit Salvation to Believers in Christ Jesus ... What therefore the Scripture has confin'd, let no Man enlarge.[66]

But the dogmatic assurance of the *Review* passage gives way to greater uncertainty and perplexity in the *Serious Reflections*: rather than confidently asserting God's favoritism toward Christians, Defoe worries about the opposite possibility, that God might look more kindly on morally upright pagans than on Christians who sin 'against saving Light'. Such paradoxes evidently intrigue him, but he abruptly abandons these theologically suspect speculations, declaring that 'I desire not to be the Promoter of unanswerable Doubts in Matters of Religion; much less would I promote Cavils at the Foundations of Religion, either as to its Profession or Practice'. At the time, 'unanswerable Doubts' of just this sort were being promoted by Deists. Their object was partly to attack as contrary to God's goodness and justice the orthodox Calvinist doctrine that only a chosen few are saved: as Tindal puts it, 'Can a Being be denominated merciful and good, who is so only to a few; but cruel, and unmerciful to the rest?'[67]

It is curious that in the passage just quoted, Defoe presents such 'Doubts' and 'Cavils' so calmly and fairly, and that instead of trying to dispel them, he abruptly resumes his gloomy geographical survey of '*the present State of* RELIGION *in the World*', in which he finds abundant grounds for 'melancholy Reflection' on the limited and beleaguered state not merely of 'RELIGION' but particularly of Christianity. The next section of this chapter, '*Of Differences in Religion*', pursues related issues in a similar spirit:

> How comes it to pass, that the paying a Reverence to the Name and Being of God, should not be as uncapable of being disputed in the Manner of it, as in the thing itself? That all the Rules of Worshipping, Believing in, and Serving the Great God of Heaven and Earth, should be capable of being understood any more than one Way? And that the Infallible Spirit of God, who is our Guide to Heaven, should leave any one of its Dictates in a State of being misunderstood?
>
> Why have not the Rules of Religion, as well those of Doctrine as of Life, been laid down in Terms so plain, and so impossible to be mistaken, that all Men in the World in every Age, should have the same Notions of them, and understand them in every Tit[t]le of them exactly alike? Then ... there would have been but one Road to travel the Journey in; all Men would have gone the same Way, steer'd the same Course; and Brethren would no more have fallen out by the Way.
>
> God alone, who for wise and righteous Reasons, because he can do nothing but what is wise and righteous, has otherwise order'd it, and that is all we can say of it: As to the Reason and Justice of it, that is a thing, of which, like as of the Times and of the Seasons, we may say, *Knoweth no Man*.[68]

Like Defoe, the Deists were fascinated by the worldwide diversity of religious beliefs and practices, but unlike Defoe they were not at all perplexed by a fact for which they had a simple, comprehensive explanation. Instead of Defoe's subdued affirmation that God's ways are inscrutable but just, the

Deists maintained that God and his purposes must be utterly reasonable, and thus readily comprehended by thoughtful men of every time and place. The proliferation of competing religions is therefore owing to the pernicious role of the clergy. Always and everywhere, priests have debased religion from its original, ideal, unitary status – as the rational worship of a benign deity and the observance of simple rules of morality – into cults based on supposed mysteries and revelations, but serving only to establish and perpetuate the wealth and power of the priests themselves. The phenomenon that puzzles and depresses Defoe is an occasion for the Deists to unveil and gloat over the scandals of priestcraft and superstition – most crucially those of Judaism and Christianity, although the ostensible objects of the Deists' satire are usually ancient pagans or overseas heathens. Once priestcraft has been identified as the historical source of all the world's ills, these become amenable to correction, by doing away with the institution responsible for them. In this respect Deism is distinctly utopian. It treats as contrary to 'nature' and 'reason' certain existing arrangements, religious and political; it suggests that firmly established as they may be, such arrangements can and should be changed drastically; and it holds out the prospect that once such modifications are brought about, mankind can expect to recover the total well-being it supposedly enjoyed in its original, natural state. For the Deists, the bogeymen were exclusively clerical and ecclesiastical, and the implications of this line of thought – of locating the source of all problems in institutions that are contingent on history and geography, and that can be altered or removed – were to be spelled out more fully by later writers like Rousseau. Yet the Deists open a clear path in this direction by abandoning, even when they do not openly repudiate, the orthodox Christian view that evil has been part of human nature since the fall. To them, evil (such as it is) is entirely contingent, the product of corrupt but replaceable institutions. On these issues, Defoe's writings and the present work belong to a somberly Augustinian, Calvinist tradition, which regards a 'Propensity to Evil rather than Good' as inborn, and reason as a fallible, inadequate bulwark against man's baser inclinations or passions.

Conclusion

Christianity Not as Old as the Creation conveys a vivid sense of the passions that could be aroused by, and the formidable theological implications that could be drawn from, such innocuous-looking Deistic propositions as that God is too merciful to want any of his creatures to be eternally miserable. This work argues forcibly against the claim in Tindal's title, that *Christian-*

ity [is] *as Old as the Creation*, but beyond this does not attempt a systematic critique of Tindal's book. Its achievement is nevertheless significant rhetorically, for it manages in effect to deny Tindal a mind or character of his own. Lumped together with 'all our Modern Despisers of *Scripture Doctrine*' (titlepage), Tindal becomes the generic Deist, whose lofty, rational pretensions mask his sinister designs against faith and morality. Other writers satirized Tindal's vices, which evidently were notorious;[69] the present work is directed against the malign tendencies of an entire movement rather than the foibles of an individual.

In fact, the scope of its irony is still more sweeping. In the *Political History of the Devil* and other works of the late 1720s, Defoe argues that instead of blaming Satan for prompting their misdeeds, people should acknowledge their own responsibility for following their vicious inclinations. Here there is a similar recognition: people are receptive to the Deists' suggestions that God is too kind and generous to punish them for vices and crimes, simply because such doctrines are so well suited to their own base appetites, not because the Deists' arguments are so powerful.[70] Satan and the Deists are deluders and betrayers, but their temptations succeed by catering to human cravings and weaknesses. This view of the world makes for irony that is broader and more effective than if its target were Tindal alone, or even the whole corps of Deists, for it embraces their willing dupes, mankind at large. If we accept this work as probably Defoe's, we can find in it fresh expressions of his crusty 'Andrew Moreton' persona, as when he affirms Westminster-Confession Calvinism by defending God's 'vindictive Attribute'. We can also gain from it new insight into his interests and actions in the last year of his life, and (not least) new evidence of his 'unwearied Application',[71] particularly if he was ill or hiding from creditors when he wrote it.

Finally, it seems worth spelling out my belief that the method used here to support the ascription of this work to Defoe could be adopted by those wishing to persuade other scholars that an anonymous book, pamphlet, or series of periodical essays is by him: namely, the preparation of an edition, the introduction and notes to which set forth the relevant evidence. Some readers of Furbank and Owens's *Defoe De-Attributions* and their *Critical Bibliography* have objected to the removal from the Defoe canon of one or another item formerly believed to be his. Several of these critics have lost sight of Furbank and Owens's argument that certain de-attributed works *could* be Defoe's, but that (because no compelling evidence for their being his has yet been produced) they should not be listed among his writings unless or until some firm support for such an attribution is forthcoming. To anyone who thinks that Furbank and Owens have mistakenly de-attributed a work that is really Defoe's, or that a work not previously associated with Defoe ought to be recognized as his, my recommendation would be that some such effort as this is called for.

Notes

1. It was '*Printed for Tho. Warner, at the Black-Boy in Pater-noster-Row*', as were various Defoe works of the 1720's, including the *Political History of the Devil* (1726), *Mere Nature Delineated* (1726), *Conjugal Lewdness* (1727), and *A New Family Instructor* (1727). Earlier in the decade Warner had been co-publisher of other major works including *Memoirs of a Cavalier* (1720), *The Life, Adventures, and Pyracies, of the famous Captain Singleton* (1720), and *The Fortunate Mistress: or, a History of ... the Lady Roxaxa* (1724).

2. Tindal's book is available in two modern editions: in the Garland series, 'British Philosophers and Theologians of the 17th and 18th Centuries', ed. René Wellek (New York, 1978), using a 432-page edition of 1730, and in the Routledge/Thoemmes series, 'History of British Deism', ed. John Vladimir Price (1995), using a 391-page edition of 1730. The 432-page and the 391-page versions are available online in ECCO; in my citations of Tindal, I supply page references to both editions.

3. 'It has been estimated that *Christianity as Old as the Creation* was the subject of 115 published replies': see S. Lalor, *Matthew Tindal, Freethinker: An Eighteenth-Century Assault on Religion* (2006), p. 17, citing Alexander Hugh Hore, *The Church of England from William III to Victoria*, 2 vols (1886), vol. 1, p. 395. In his Introduction to the Routledge/Thoemmes Press reprint of *Christianity as Old as the Creation*, p. ix, John Valdimir Price says that 'Over the next decade, the work prompted, in one form or another, over one hundred and fifty replies, from sermons and pamphlets to learned theological treatises and scholarly analyses'. In the *Oxford DNB* life of Tindal, B. W. Young says, 'In all, something like thirty replies, from pamphlets to quartos, appeared to repudiate its message'. Young's figure may be based on the British Museum *Catalogue of Printed Books*, which lists nearly forty replies (cols 10–13); I do not know the basis for Hore's or Price's.

4. On the subject of internal evidence, it may be helpful to quote their sensible remarks:

> One important class of such evidence will be close resemblance to the author's known works, especially close verbal resemblance or unacknowledged quotation, but also close similarity in regard to some idiosyncratic train of thought. Internal evidence, to be convincing, is likely to consist of more than one piece, and a stylistic resemblance can be strengthened as evidence by known facts about the author ... we regard it as legitimate in attribution to pay regard to favourite *allusions* (anecdotes, historical references, legendary stories and the like) and also to favourite quota-

tions. Defoe had many favourite and idiosyncratic allusions ... and it seems perverse not to allow them a certain weight as internal evidence. How much weight is a difficult question and will depend very much on the context and on how many of them there are in a given work; at best they are a relatively weak prop to an ascription, but sometimes they are all, or almost all, that one has to go on.

P. N. Furbank and W. R. Owens, *A Critical Bibliography of Daniel Defoe* (1998), pp. xxvi–xxvii.

5.   'These letters [to his daughter and son-in-law] show Defoe in a time of physical and psychological exhaustion. He was in pain and no longer able to write': see Maximillian E. Novak, 'Defoe as a Biographical Subject', *Literature Compass*, 3 (2006), pp. 1218–34, at p. 1230.

6.   See G. A. Starr, '"Sauces to whet our gorg'd Appetites": Defoe at Seventy in the Anchovy Trade', *Philological Quarterly*, 54:2 (1975), pp. 531–3; cf. also Paula R. Backscheider, *Daniel Defoe: His Life* (Baltimore, 1989), p. 606.

7.   One more or less complete and one unfinished work remained in manuscript at his death, but it appears that he was involved with them no later than 1729, rather than in his final year. See Furbank and Owens, *Critical Bibliography*, items 270, 'The Compleat English Gentleman' ['1728–9'], and 271, 'Of Royall Educacion' ['1727?'].

8.   *Christianity as Old as the Creation* was advertised in the *Daily Journal* and the *Daily Post* for 7 April 1730, and *The Country Journal or The Craftsman* for 11 April 1730. The *Monthly Chronicle* lists it among books published in April 1730 (Vol. 3, p. 86, item 76); the same source gives *Christianity Not as Old as the Creation* as a May 1730 publication (p. 108, item 74). The earliest '*This Day is Published*' listing I have found for *Christianity Not as Old as the Creation* is in *The Country Journal or The Craftsman* for 13 June 1730. Whether it appeared three weeks or six weeks after *Christianity as Old as the Creation*, this work found its way into print rapidly. Defoe was 'noted', as one contemporary put it, 'for the Expeditiousness of his Pen': see *Grumbler*, 14 (3–6 May 1715).

9.   This question was added to the reprinting of George Chalmers's 1786 *Life of Defoe* in Defoe's *Works*, 20 vols (Oxford, 1841), vol. 20, p. 87; at this time it was supposed that Defoe's last published work, 'under the assumed name of Andrew Moreton', was *Second Thoughts are Best*, 1729.

10. See *A Brief State of the Inland or Home Trade, of England*, listed in Furbank and Owens, *A Critical Bibliography of Daniel Defoe*, item 249(P), p. 241; like the present work, it was '*Printed for Tho. Warner, at the Black-Boy in Pater-noster-Row*'.

11. Part II consists of 'INSTRUCTIONS against the THREE GRAND ERRORS of the TIMES; Viz. 1. Asserting the *Divine Authority* of the SCRIPTURE; against the DEISTS. 2. PROOFS, that the MESSIAS is already come, *&c.* against the ATHEISTS and JEWS. 3. Asserting, the DIVINITY of JESUS CHRIST ... against our MODERN HERETICKS': see the title page of *A New Family Instructor*, in

Religious and Didactic Writings, vol. 3. Such targets were seen as related, and were often aimed at within single works; thus the subtitle of Theophilus Lobb's *Discourse on Ministerial Instruction* (1712) reads, *Wherein, the Being of a God Against the Atheists; The Divine Authority of the Scriptures Against the Deists; The Doctrine of the Trinity against the Socinians, are briefly Dicuss'd.* Part of the subtitle of John Edwards's *Theologia Reformata* (1713) says the work is '*design'd as an Antidote in this Corrupted Age against the dangerous Opinions of* Papists, Arians *and* Socinians, Pelagians *and* Remonstrants, Anabaptists, Antinomians, Deists, Atheists, Scepticks, Enthusiasts, Libertines'.

12. See David Berman, 'Matthew Tindal', in *The Encyclopedia of Unbelief*, ed. G. Stein, 2 vols (Buffalo, 1985), vol. 2, pp. 666–70; Stephen S. Lalor, 'Matthew Tindal', in *The Dictionary of Eighteenth-Century British Philosophers*, ed. John W. Yolton, John Valdimir Price and J. Stephens, 2 vols (Bristol, 1999), vol. 2, pp. 876–80; Lalor's more recent *Matthew Tindal, Freethinker: An Eighteenth-Century Assault on Religion* (2006), pp. 111–40; and the excellent chapter on 'The True Religion of Nature: the Freethinkers and their Opponents', in Isabel Rivers, *Reason, Grace, and Sentiment: A Study of the Language of Religion and Ethics in England, 1660–1780*, vol. 2 (Cambridge, 2000), esp. pp. 76–84. Wayne Hudson discusses Tindal in *The English Deists: Studies in Early Enlightenment* (2009), pp. 106–13, and in *Enlightenment and Modernity: The English Deists and Reform* (2009), pp. 34–47. Other accounts include Richard H. Popkin, 'The Deist Challenge', in *From Persecution to Toleration: The Glorious Revolution and Religion in England*, ed. Ole Peter Grell, Jonathan I. Israel and Nicholas Tyacke (Oxford, 1991), pp. 195–215; James A. Herrick, *The Radical Rhetoric of the English Deists: The Discourse of Skepticism, 1680–1750* (Columbia, South Carolina, 1997); James M. Byrne, 'The Distant God of Deism', in *Religion and the Enlightenment From Descartes to Kant* (Louisville, 1997), pp. 99–123; Chapters 3 and 4 of Peter Byrne, *Natural Religion and the Nature of Religion: The Legacy of Deism* (1989), pp. 52–110. Jeffrey R. Wigelsworth's *Deism in Enlightenment England: Theology, Politics and Newtonian Public Science* (Manchester, 2009) contains an extensive and useful bibliography. Of unusual interest is Justin Champion's *Republican Learning: John Toland and the Crisis of Christian Culture, 1696–1722* (Manchester, 2003), and his earlier *The Pillars of Priestcraft Shaken: The Church of England and its Enemies, 1660–1730* (Cambridge, 1992). Still provocative is Leslie Stephen's discussion of 'Tindal and his Opponents', in *History of English Thought in the Eighteenth Century* (1876), 2 vols (1927); among other early studies, see the entry on Deism by G. C. Joyce in the *Encyclopædia of Religion and Ethics*, ed. James Hastings (1911), vol. 4, pp. 533–43, and the relevant sections of J. Orr, *English Deism: Its Roots and Its Fruits* (Grand Rapids, 1934).

13. See the *Review* (12 November 1706), quoting [James Hodges], *The Rights and Interests Of the British Monarchies* (1706); in the preceding number of the *Review* (9 November 1706), Defoe had said Hodges could legitimately

'reproach us ... with the Connivence in *England* at *Deism, Socinianism* ... and the like Errors, not taken Cognizance of by the Church of *England*'.

14. These examples are all from the *Serious Reflections*, in *Novels*, vol. 3, pp. 113, 200, 237, 172, 201; they could be multiplied from other works of the decade.

15. Although Defoe constantly associates Deism with atheism, he does not simply equate them. In the *Serious Reflections*, in *Novels*, vol. 3, p. 118, this paragraph on the Deists follows one on outright atheists:

> Below these we have a Sort of People who will acknowledge a God, but he must be such a one as they please to make him; a fine well bred good natur'd Gentleman like Deity, that cannot have the Heart to damn any of his Creatures to an Eternal Punishment, nor could not be so weak as to let the *Jews* crucify his own Son; these Men expose Religion, and all the Doctrines of Repentance, and Faith in Christ, with all the Means of a Christian Salvation, as matter of Banter and Ridicule. The Bible they say is a good History in most Parts, but the Story of our Saviour they look upon as a meer Novel, and the Miracles of the New Testament as a Legend of Priestcraft.

16. In 'Defoe, the Occult, and the Deist Offensive during the Reign of George I', in *Deism, Masonry, and the Enlightenment: Essays Honoring Alfred Owen Aldridge*, ed. J. A. Leo Lemay (Newark, Delaware, 1987), p. 94, Maximillian E. Novak argues that Defoe 'was responding mainly to a group of writers on religious subjects who, starting with John Toland's *Nazarenus* in 1718 and ending with Anthony Collins's *The Scheme of Literal Prophecy Considered*, in 1727, raised questions about the origins of Christianity and the doctrines associated with the teachings of Christ'. Defoe was no doubt familiar with the writers Prof. Novak mentions, but his critiques of Deism span several decades, treat various other issues, and seldom refer by name to specific authors or works.

17. See *Serious Reflections*, in *Novels*, vol. 3, p. 135:

> where-ever Christianity has been planted or profess'd nationally in the World, even where it has not had a *Saving* Influence, it has yet had a *Civilizing* Influence: It has operated upon the Manners, the Morals, the Politics, and even the Tempers and Dispositions of the People: It has reduc'd them to the Practice of Virtue, and to the true Methods of Living, has wean'd them from the *Barbarous* Customs they had been used to, infusing a Kind of Humanity and Softness of Disposition into their very Natures; civilizing and softning them, teaching them to love a Regularity of Life, and filling them with Principles of generous Kindness and Beneficence one to another; in a Word, it has taught them to live like Men, and act upon the Foundations of Clemency, Humanity, Love, and good Neighbourhood.

Cf. also the *Farther Adventures*, in *Novels*, vol. 2, p. 159, apropos of Taiwan, where Dutch missionaries had once been active: 'the Christian Religion always civilizes the People, and reforms their Manners, where it is receiv'd, whether it works saving Effects upon them or no'.

18. *Christianity as Old as the Creation*, 391-page edn, p. 367; 432-page edn, p. 406.
19. *Christianity as Old as the Creation*, 391-page edn., p. 366; 432-page edn, p. 404. On this subject see Eric Sean Nelson, 'Leibniz and China: Religion, Hermeneutics, and Enlightenment', in *Religion in the Age of Enlightenment*, ed. Brett C. McInelly (New York, 2009), vol. 1, pp. 279–302.
20. See p. 60 below.
21. 'They ... bring the Deity ... under such Regulations and Restrictions, that they scarce allow him to be a GOD at all. They will have him be so good, so merciful, so beneficent, that he cannot be Just': see *A New Family Instructor*, in *Religious and Didactic Writings,* vol. 3, p. 204. The Deists divest him of 'all Resentment against the vilest Offences: robbing him of the Power of Rewards and Punishments, and making him so good, so kind and gracious, that they do not leave him room to be Just': see *A System of Magick*, in *Satire, Fantasy and Writings on the Supernatural*, Vol. 7, p. 182. And they treat God as 'a fine well bred good natur'd Gentleman like Deity, that cannot have the Heart to damn any of his Creatures to an Eternal Punishment': see *Serious Reflections*, in *Novels*, vol. 3, p.101.
22. See D. P. Walker, *The Decline of Hell* (Chicago, 1964), and Philip C. Almond, *Heaven and Hell in Enlightenment England* (Cambridge, 1994).
23. The most influential statement of this view at the time is Shaftesbury's, in 'An Inquiry concerning Virtue', in *Characteristicks of Men, Manners, Opinions, Times*, ed. Philip Ayres, 2 vols (Oxford, 1999), vol. 1, p. 199; we do not say that someone 'is *a good Man*, when having his Hands ty'd up, he is hinder'd from doing the Mischief he designs; or (which is in a manner the same) when he abstains from executing his ill purpose, thro a fear of some impending Punishment, or thro the allurement of some exteriour Reward'. Moreover,

> If ... there be a Belief or Conception of a DEITY, who is consider'd only as ... inforcing Obedience to his *absolute Will* by particular Rewards and Punishments; and if on this account, thro Hope merely of *Reward*, or Fear of *Punishment,* the Creature be incited to do the Good he hates, or restrain'd from doing the Ill to which he is not otherwise in the least degree averse; there is in this Case ... no Virtue or Goodness whatsoever. The Creature, notwithstanding his good Conduct, is intrinsically of as little Worth, as if he acted in his natural way, when under no Dread or Terror of any sort. There is no more of *Rectitude, Piety*, or *Sanctity* in a Creature thus reform'd, than there is *Meekness* or *Gentleness* in a Tyger strongly chain'd, or *Innocence* and *Sobriety* in a Monkey under the Discipline of the Whip (vol. 1, pp. 215–16).

Expressions of the belief that virtue is its own reward, by followers of Shaftesbury such as John Toland (1670–1722), John Trenchard (1668/9–

1723), and Thomas Gordon(d. 1750), are cited by J. A. I. Champion in
The Pillars of Priestcraft Shaken, p. 216, n. 51.

24. See the references assembled in explanatory note 152 below.

25. This and the next three quotations are from *A New Family Instructor*, in *Religious and Didactic Writings*, Vol. 3, p. 204.

26. 'What Notions must the Vulgar have of God ... when they find he is said to be *jealous* and *furious*? And God himself says, *My Fury shall come up in my Face, for in my Jealousy, and in th Fire of my Wrath have I spoken* [Ezekiel 38:19–29]; with a Number of other Expressions of the like Nature? Nay, does not the Scripture ... suppose, that God does Things of the greatest Moment in Anger and Fury?' (*Christianity as Old as the Creation*, 432-page edn, p. 251, 391-page edn., p. 226).

27. See Shaftesbury, 'An Inquiry concerning Virtue', in *Characteristicks*, vol. 1, p. 212, quoted by Tindal, 432-page edn., p. 74, 391-page edn., p. 63.

28. See *Christianity as Old as the Creation*, 432-page edn., p. 78, 391-page edn., p. 67. Here too Tindal has Calvinist Christianity in mind, as did Shaftesbury in declaring that 'we know very well that, in some Religions, there are those who expressly give no other Idea of GOD, than of a Being arbitrary, violent, causing ill, and ordaining to Misery, which in effect is the same as to substitute a DÆMON, or *Devil*, in his room': see 'An Inquiry concerning Virtue', in *Characteristicks*, vol. 1, p. 195. In *The Eternity of Hell Torments Considered* (1740), pp. 18–19, William Whiston similarly contrasts 'the Love of God to mankind' with 'these common but barbarous and savage opinions' of his punitiveness, according to which 'the greater part of mankind ... must inevitably be damned ... [to] exquisite torments ... without abatement, or remission for endless ages of ages ... without any other advantage to themselves, or to others, or to God himself, than as instances ... of the absolute and supreme power and dominion of the cruel and inexorable author of their being'.

29. In *A New Family Instructor*, the father declares,

> It is very true, they would have a GOD without a Devil, according to *Epicurus*; a GOD Wise and Powerful, but not infinitely so, not Omnipotent, not Self-sufficient, and All-sufficient; a GOD that having created the World (and 'tis with some Difficulty they go so far) has not Power to guide it, but has abandoned it to the Government of it self; to that foolish *Nothing*, that unexisting Piece of Nonsense, call'd *Chance*; or like the Followers of *Zeno* that Deist Philosopher, a God depending upon (they know not what, of a) blind Destiny; a God who not being able to break the Chain of second Causes, is carry'd away with them himself, being obliged to act by the Course of natural Consequences, even whether he will or no.

See *A New Family Instructor*, in *Religious and Didactic Writings*, vol. 3, p. 209

30. See *A New Family Instructor*, in *Religious and Didactic Writings*, vol. 3, p. 200.
31. See *Compleat English Gentleman*, in *Religious and Didactic Writings*, vol. 10, p. 43; cf. also *The Poor Man's Plea*, in *Religious and Didactic Writings*, vol. 6, ed. J. A. Downie (2007), p. 31; *Serious Reflections*, in *Novels*, vol. 3, p.179 and n. 508, p. 376.
32. See *The Universal Passion. Satire VI. On Women* (1728), pp. 22–3.
33. See *The Sixth Epistle of the First Book of Horace Imitated* (1737), ll. 63–6, in *Imitations of Horace*, ed. J. Butt, in *The Twickenham Edition of the Poems of Alexander Pope* (London & New Haven, 1961), vol. 4, p. 241.
34. Elsewhere Pope's lines on 'Toland and Tindal, prompt at Priests to jeer' similarly satirize Tindal's disdain for all churches and clergies, and his hostility toward Christianity itself: see *The Dunciad*, II, l. 367, ed. James Sutherland, in *The Twickenham Edition of the Poems of Alexander Pope* (London & New Haven, 1953), vol. 5, p. 144.
35. See *Novels*, vol. 3, pp. 116–17. In the Preface to *The Storm*, Defoe leads up to these verses with similar ruminations (sig. [A6^{recto}-A6^{verso}]):

    Certainly Atheism is one of the most Irrational Principles in the World; there is something incongruous in it with the Test of Humane Policy, because there is a Risque in the Mistake one way, and none another. If the Christian is mistaken, and it should at last appear that there is no Future State, God or Devil, Reward or Punishment, where is the Harm of it? All he has lost is, that he … took the pains to live a little more like a Man than he wou'd have done. But if the Atheist is mistaken, he has brought all the Powers, whose Being he deny'd, upon his Back … and must at last sink under the Anger of him whose Nature he has always disown'd. I would recommend this Thought to any Man to consider of, one Way he can loose nothing, the other he may be undone. Certainly a wise Man would never run such an unequal Risque.

36. See *Novels*, vol. 3, p. 264.
37. It has become something of a critical commonplace that Defoe's favourite poet was Rochester, although this is a calculation based more on frequency of citation than effusiveness of praise, which would probably put Milton ahead of Rochester. But if we are to judge such matters by frequency of citation, then Defoe's favourite poet, by far, is not Rochester but Defoe. In the *Serious Reflections*, Defoe cites Rochester twice, other poets five times, and himself (I believe) twenty times … Throughout his writings he quotes verse widely, sometimes citing his source, sometimes not, seldom using pre-seventeenth-century poetry, but most commonly his own, as if its gnomic crispness and vigour entitled it to the same authority as the classics.
    See *Serious Reflections*, in *Novels*, Vol. 3, Introduction, p. 8; on Defoe's fondness for Rochester, see John McVeagh, 'Rochester and Defoe: A Study in Influence', *Studies In English Literature*, 14 (1974), pp. 327–42.

38. See 'A Letter concerning Enthusiasm', in *Characteristicks*, vol. 1, p. 23.
39. These points are developed at greatest length in the *Political History of the Devil* and *A System of Magick*, but arise elsewhere as well: see above, p. xvii, on this passage. In *Christianity as Old as the Creation*, Tindal calls Satan a 'subtle and malignant Spirit, endow'd with an universal Knowledge of what is past, and *a deep Penetration into Futurity*' (391-page edn., p. 351; 432-page edn., p. 388; italics added).
40. See pp. 6, 46 below; cf. also p. 49 below, where the same point is made for the third time: 'To what End do Men strain their Wits to find Flaws in the Translation, and to form Objections, and seeming Contradictions in the several Versions, while they cannot undermine or destroy the Foundation?'. In *A New Family Instructor*, Defoe is similarly harsh toward unbelievers who,

    leaving the plain and undeniable Consequences of Things, and turning or wresting the Scriptures to their own particular Meanings, would ... seek for Shifts and Subterfuges in the different Readings, and doubtful ambiguous Construction of Words to avoid the Force of plain and pungent Texts; so to lessen the Credit of them, or leave us unsatisfied of the true Sense, till they can decide those jarring Disputes, reconcile those Readings, and have all their Objections answered and silenced, which may probably never be brought to pass.

    See *A New Family Instructor*, in *Religious and Didactic Writings*, vol. 3, p. 267.
41. Among pretensions to self-sufficiency, the most extreme was the denial that God created the world or man. This position was often attacked as a revival of pagan notions – either that the world is eternal, and had no beginning, or that the world did have a beginning, but that this was owing to a random concourse of pre-existing atoms rather than to any creative agent. Here Epicurus is identified with 'the Doctrine of the Eternity of the World', which is called 'a Notion too gross to deserve a reply, and too ridiculous to bring it into a Discourse so solemn and serious as this' (p. 41). Defoe refers critically to Epicurus in at least three works, but associates him with the 'Notion' that the world came into being 'by meer Chance, by a fortuitous Conjunction of Atoms', rather than with the theory that it had no beginning (see below, explanatory note 113 to p. 41). On the face of it, this might seem a piece of evidence against Defoe's authorship of the present work. The difference, however, may be mainly one of emphasis, since Defoe's contemporaries evidently regarded the '*Self-existent, Independent and Eternal*' qualities of atoms as integral (but equally absurd) aspects of the Epicurean theory: see the quotation from Sir Richard Blackmore's *Creation* in explanatory note 113 below. For evidence that critics of the day regarded Epicurus as holding or implying 'that each atom has existed from eternity', see J. J. Macintosh, 'Robert Boyle on Epicurean atheism and atomism', in *Atoms,*

pneuma, *and tranquillity*, ed. Margaret J. Osler (Cambridge, 1991), p. 211 and *passim*.

42. Defoe's habit of citing Scripture, sometimes incongruously and inaccurately but usually (I believe) 'without Book', is discussed in my 'Defoe and Biblical Memory', in *New Windows on a Woman's World: A Festschrift for Jocelyn Harris*, ed. Colin Gibson and Lisa Marr (Dunedin, 2006), pp. 316–35. The sheer abundance of Biblical references in the present work points strongly to a non-Church of England author; the liberties taken with the text are characteristically Defoean. For instance, 1 Timothy 1:15 is cited (p. 46 below) as '*It is a faithful saying, and worthy of all acceptation*', as if Scripture were the antecedent of '*It*', and the apostle's intention was to defend Scripture as the word of God. Yet the passage actually reads, 'This is a faithful saying, and worthy of all acceptation, that Christ Jesus came into the world to save sinners; of whom I am chief'; cf. also p. 00 [53] below, where St Paul is again represented as upholding the authority of Scripture at large. More bizarre is a Biblical image introduced in a discussion of the problem of original sin; the author poses the rhetorical question, 'how came it into the Man? How had this Legion Power to enter into the Herd?' (p. 41 below). The allusion is to Luke 8:27–33, where Christ allows the devils to leave a man and enter a herd of swine. As a metaphor for crime first entering mankind, this is amusingly far-fetched (or heretical, if taken seriously), but so are many of Defoe's Biblical citations.

43. Instead of quoting Rochester *against* the Deists, pious writers tended to associate Rochester *with* them, as in G[eorge] Benson's pamphlet, *The End and Design of Prayer, Or, The Reasonableness of praying to an unchangeably Wise, Powerful, and Good God. In Answer to the Objections of the late Earl of Rochester, Mr. Blount, My Lord Shaftesbury, and other modern Deists* (1730), p. 6, where Rochester is cited from Gilbert Burnet's *Some Passages of the Life and Death Of the Right Honourable John, Earl of Rochester* (1680 and many later edns.).

44. See pp. 10–11 below: 'How many great Men have we seen endowed with the utmost Perfection of human Knowledge; yet groveling in the Dark, and producing the most monstrous Errors, and even Absurdities in the sublimest Parts of Science, and such as are best fitted for Contemplation?'

45. See *Writings on Travel, Discovery and History*, vol. 5.

46. See *The Storm* (1704), pp. 2, 10: 'where we see Effects but cannot reach their Causes ... Nature plainly refers us beyond her Self, to the mighty Hand of Infinite Power, the Author of Nature, and Original of all Causes ... Other things are left to the Common Discoveries of natural Inquiry, but this [the wind] is a thing he holds in his own Hand, and has conceal'd from the Search of the most Diligent and Piercing Understanding'; cf. also *A Journal of the Plague Year*, in *Novels*, vol. 7, Introduction, pp. 11–17..

47. See *Serious Reflections*, in *Novels*, Vol. 3, p. 186.

48. In *The Enlightenment and religion: The Myths of Modernity* (Manchester, 2003), S. J. Barnett goes a step beyond this, contending that Deism was more a 'myth'

than a 'movement', contrived at the time as a 'scare' for political purposes. Barnett represents the Church of England opponents of Deism as mere careerists who 'wished to make a name for themselves by publicly appearing as staunch defenders of the faith and thus bringing themselves to the notice of their superiors'; he declares that 'In an effort to promote their own sects, dissenting propagandists were also inclined to exaggerate rather than minimize threats to Christianity as proof that the Anglican Church-state alliance was leading to iniquity'; and he concludes that 'the illusion that was eighteenth-century deism was to some degree a media production' (pp. 68–9). In my opinion, Barnett slips into the same polemical exaggerations and distortions that he sees in the original adversaries and the modern commentators on Deism.

49. See the *Review,* 16 September 1704; *Supplement,* November 1704, pp. 558–60; the relevant passage is quoted above, p. xlviii.

50. See *The Mock Mourners* (in *Poetry,* in *Satire, Fantasy and Writings on the Supernatural,* vol. 1, p.143, ll. 232–3): 'In vain they strive with Bravery to appear, / For where there's Guilt, there always will be Fear'; *The Spanish Descent* (in *Poetry,* in *Satire, Fantasy and Writings on the Supernatural,* vol. 1, p. 200, ll. 195–6): 'His Constant Temper's all Serene and Clear; / First free from Guilt, and therefore free from Fear'; *The Dyet of Poland* (in *Poetry,* in *Satire, Fantasy and Writings on the Supernatural,* vol. 1, p. 359, ll. 524–5): 'Courage and Crime can never dwell so near, / For where there's *Guilt,* there always will be *Fear'.* Defoe uses the line with minor variants in *Ye True-Born Englishmen Proceed* (in *Poetry,* in *Satire, Fantasy and Writings on the Supernatural,* vol. 1, p. 129, ll. 134–5); cf. also *Serious Reflections,* in *Novels,* vol. 3, p. 104; *History and Reality of Apparitions,* in *Satire, Fantasy and Writings on the Supernatural,* vol. 8, p. 257. Defoe makes a similar point in *Reformation of Manners*: 'Nothing but Guilt can be the Cause of Fear', l. 422 (in *Poetry,* in *Satire, Fantasy and Writings on the Supernatural,* vol. 1, p. 168); for more expressions of the same sentiment, see G. A. Starr, *Defoe and Casuistry* (Princeton, 1971), p. 178, n. 20.

51. See the *Political History of the Devil,* in *Satire, Fantasy and Writings on the Supernatural,* vol. 6, p. 102: 'thus encroaching Crime dethrones the Sense, ... Debauches Reason, makes the Man a Fool, / And turns his active light to Ridicule'; Defoe is adapting verses from his *Jure Divino* (1706), Book 7, ll. 123–6, in *Satire, Fantasy and Writings on the Supernatural,* vol. 2, p. 220, where he says in a note, 'Sin makes us all Fools, and nothing falters in Speech, and betrays it self by its Inconsistencies and Nonsense, like a detected Criminal, with Guilt in his Face'.

52. See the passages from the *Political History of the Devil* quoted on p. xvi above. P. N. Furbank speaks of 'a leading trait of his, a lack of all capacity for awe. He is habitually facetious about Biblical characters – about Adam, 'that effeminated Male Apple-Eater; the she-tyrant Eve; and Noah, the first of Drunkards': see *A General History of Discoveries and Improvements,* in *Writings on Travel, Dis-*

covery and History, vol. 4, Introduction, p. 11; on Defoe's 'habitual tendency towards facetiousness when discussing Biblical stories', and Adam and Eve in particular, see also W. R. Owens, *Poetry*, in *Satire, Fantasy and Writings on the Supernatural*, vol. 1, Introduction, p. 34.

53. A typical expression of this deference-deficient habit of mind is Defoe's mini-sequel to *Paradise Lost*, a dramatization of Cain succumbing to Satan's wiles and determining to kill Abel: see the *Political History of the Devil*, in *Satire, Fantasy and Writings on the Supernatural*, vol. 6, pp. 106–11.

54. Several of his fictional characters conduct themselves toward readers as if they were defendants before judges and juries (as some of them literally are, on occasion). Here the presentation of Adam as if on trial in court does not point unequivocally toward Defoe as author, but provides another suggestive affinity, both substantive and stylistic, to his known works. Specimens of courtroom jargon include, 'when GOD called him, and he was forc'd to come forth and hold up his Hand, as we might call it, what did he do? He came trembling, pleaded guilty, confest the Indictment ... but talk'd like a Fool' (see p. 40 below). Legal imagery extends from general words like 'Sentence', 'Pardon', and 'Execution' to more specific terms of art such as to 'plead ... in arrest of judgment' (see p. 53 below), and 'the Testimony of Scripture ... admitted in Evidence on the Trial of the Cases before us' (see p. 47 below).

55. See *Christianity as Old as the Creation*, 432-page edn, p. 390; 391-page edn, p. 353.

56. See *Christianity as Old as the Creation*, 432-page edn, pp. 385–6; 391-page edn, p. 349.

57. See *A New Discovery of an Old Intreague* (1691), ll.61–4, in *Poetry*, in *Satire, Fantasy and Writings on the Supernatural*, vol. 1, p. 51.

58. See the *Serious Reflections*, in *Novels*, vol. 3, p. 228.

59. See the *Family Instructor I*, in *Religious and Didactic Writings*, vol. 1, p. 59. In the second volume of the same work, this principle is reaffirmed: 'no doubt, Nature is vitiated and tainted with several Infirmities, whether originally, and by Descent from the first Man, is not our present Subject, but so it is; there are powerful Inclinations to do Evil in every one, which we can give very little account of': see the *Family Instructor II*, in *Religious and Didactic Writings*, vol. 2, p. 132.

60. On the Dissenters' doctrinal agreement with the Church of England, Defoe says in the *Review* (25 September 1705), 'I freely subscribe to all her [the Church of England's] Doctrinal Articles, and so do the General Body of all the *Dissenters* in *England*. The Difference principally lies in what Mr. *L*[es]*ly* calls the Regale and Pontificate in Ceremonies, the Episcopal Hierarchy, and the Power of the Civil Magistrate in Imposing and making Indifferent things Necessary'.

61. Defoe seems to have had misgivings about this tenet of Calvinism, and a passage in the present work appears to be making a sly joke at its expense. After the fall, Adam 'had all the Reason in the World to believe, that what the just and holy

Majesty of God had pronounced with so much solemn Asseveration, should be fulfilled, and that he should *surely die*. Whence then had he any Comfort? Whence did he learn that God had pitied his Misery and would not destroy him, tho' he had deserv'd it, and God had threatned it? nay, had, as we say, decreed it, tho', as it appear'd, not unalterably' (see pp. 38–9 below). This is a play on words, because the Calvinist point about God's decrees is precisely that they *are* unalterable: in the words of the Westminster Assembly's *Confession of Faith*, 'Of God's Eternal Decree', God has 'unchangeably ordain[ed] whatsoever comes to pass' (Chap. 3, ¶).

62. See John Robert Moore, *Daniel Defoe: Citizen of the Modern World* (Chicago, 1958), which celebrates Defoe as pioneer and prophet of the new, not as someone interested in preserving or perpetuating anything old.

63. See *Christianity as Old as the Creation*, 432-page edn., pp. 388–9; 391-page edn, p. 352; in the same vein, cf. Shaftesbury's remark that 'not to correct, or totally exclude that Ill of Chance, or of a contrary ill Design, must proceed either from *Impotency*, or *Ill-Will*': 'An Inquiry concerning Virtue', *Characteristicks of Men, Manners, Opinions, Times*, vol. 1, p. 193.

64. See vol. 1, p. 221. Defoe nevertheless shares one of the Deists' key convictions, regarding the dispensability of priests for the attaining of religious knowledge. Thus Crusoe declares (vol. 1, p. 220),

> How infinite and inexpressible a Blessing it is, that the Knowledge of God, and of the Doctrine of Salvation by *Jesus Christ*, is so plainly laid down in the Word of God; so easy to be receiv'd and understood: That as the bare reading the Scripture made me capable of understanding enough of my Duty, to carry me directly on to the great Work of sincere Repentance for my sins, and laying hold of a Saviour for Life and Salvation, to a stated Reformation in Practice, and Obedience to all God's Commands, and this without any Teacher or Instructor; I mean, humane; so the same plain Instruction sufficiently serv'd to the enlightning this Savage Creature, and bringing him to be such a Christian, as I have known few equal to him in my Life.

> In such passages, however, Defoe's belief that truth can be attained without the help of priests springs from a traditional Protestant commitment to the principle of *sola scriptura*, whereas the Deists are intent on doing away with the authority of the Bible along with that of the priesthood. On this issue see the *Westminster Confession of Faith*, Chap.1, ¶ 7: 'All things in scripture are not alike plain in themselves, nor alike clear unto all; yet those things which are necessary to be known, believed, and observed, for salvation, are so clearly propounded and opened in some place of scripture or other, that not only the learned, but the unlearned, in a due use of the ordinary means, may attain unto a sufficient understanding of them'.

65. See *Serious Reflections*, in *Novels*, vol. 3, pp. 133–4.

66. See *Review*, 16 September 1704; *Supplement*, November 1704, pp. 558–60.

67. See *Christianity as Old as the Creation*, 432-page edn., p. 401; 391-page edn.,
    p. 363; more consistent with divine beneficence, according to the Deists, is
    '*That God, at all Times, has given Mankind sufficient Means of knowing what
    he requires of them*'; see *Christianity as Old as the Creation*, in which this is the
    title or argument of the first chapter. Thus the religion of nature, which con-
    tains everything necessary to the welfare of mankind, now or hereafter, has been
    available, always and everywhere, to wise pagans no less than to Christians.

68. See *Serious Reflections*, in *Novels*, vol. 3, pp. 158–9.

69. B. W. Young points out that 'Tindal's reputation for sensual indulgence, both
    sexual and at the table, was often used against him', and that he 'was publicly rep-
    rimanded at All Souls as "an Egregious Fornicator" (*Oxford DNB*). According
    to Abel Evans, 'In *Vice* and *Error* from his *Cradle* Nurs'd', Tindal 'Studies hard,
    and takes extreme Delight, / In Whores, or Heresies to spend the Night': see
    The Apparation (1710), p. 6. See also [Thomas Newcomb], *Blasphemy As Old as
    the Creation ... A satyr. Address'd to the Modern Advocates of Irreligion, Prophane-
    ness, and Infidelity* (1730); Tindal is called '*A modern Epicurean Philosopher,
    very remarkable for his good Eating, and bad Principles*' (p. 8).

70. the Presumption, that God is so good that he cannot resent ... tends to
    raze out the fear of God from the Minds of Men, and leave every Man to
    walk in his own Ways, being a Rule to himself; For if the Goodness and
    Beneficence of God is such ... that he will take no notice of our Offences
    ... what Inference is more rational than this, that then every Man may live
    as he pleases? As when there was no King in *Israel*, every Man did what
    was right in his own Eyes, so when we can perswade our selves, that there
    are no Thunders in Heaven, no Vengeance to be fear'd from thence, we
    shall all do the like (p. 55 below).

71. See p. 9 below. For Defoe's admiration of 'unwearied Application', see *A Brief
    State of the Inland or Home Trade, of England*, p. 6; *Letters Written by a Turk-
    ish Spy*, in *Satire, Fantasy and Writings on the Supernatural*, vol. 5, p. 78. For
    his similar appreciation of 'indefatigable Application' see *A General History of
    Discoveries and Improvements*, in *Writings on Travel, Discovery and History*, vol.
    4, p. 174; *Plan of the English Commerce*, in *Political and Economic Writings*, vol.
    7, p. 285; *Serious Reflections*, in *Novels*, vol. 3, p. 53.

ぞぞぞぞぞぞぞぞぞぞ

CHRISTIANITY

NOT as Old as the

CREATION, *&c.*

ぞぞぞぞぞぞぞぞぞぞぞ

CHRISTIANITY

NOT *as Old as the* CREATION:

BEING AN

ESSAY

UPON THE

Original of *Divine Revelation.*

SHEWING

That RELIGION can only Subsist upon

a Divine *Revelation.*

Which may serve for

A SHORT but FULL ANSWER to

Mr. *TBd--ll's Christianity*, &c.

And to all our **Modern Despisers** of *Scripture*

Doctrine.

WITH AN

APPENDIX

Affectionately address'd to the YOUTH of

this AGE; to prevent, if possible, their

being debauch'd with Atheistic and Deistic

PRINCIPLES.

LONDON:

Printed for T. WARNER, at the *Black Boy* in

Pater-Noster-Row. 1730. [Price 1 *s.*]

AN

ESSAY

UPON THE

Nature and Original of Divine Revelation.

CHAP. I.

Of the several Attempts, made by mistaken Men, against the Establish'd Doctrine of Revelation.

REVEALED RELIGION is a Fortification so strong, that it requires a very Numerous Artillery to beat it down, and such our Adversaries think they have prepared against it. We shall soon try the Strength of their Engines of all Sorts.

The Enemies of God, for such I must take all those to be who thus refuse, as the Scripture says, *him that speaketh from Heaven*, Heb. xii.25. have levell'd their Batteries against this Voice from Heaven in two several Places, and I must confess they have aim'd them right, for if they could overthrow the Outworks on that Side, they would shake the very Foundation of all Religion.

They have, I say, made a right Judgment on one Hand, namely, that this is the only thing they can do to overthrow the whole Scheme of our Holy Religion, and that it is in vain to attack us in any other Quarter.

But withal they have shewn the Weakness of their Skill, and that they could not see, that Reveal'd Religion (to carry on the Allegory) is impregnable; that it is impossible to shake the Foundation on which it stands; namely, the Sacred and Written Word; that it is a Building fram'd in Heaven, and out of their reach, of which Jesus Christ himself *is the chief corner Stone*.[1]

Let us then look a little into the Pretences they make, for blessed be God they are no more than Pretences.

1. They at once reject all Scripture-Evidence. And this they think is a *Coup d'Eclat*,[2] a mortal Blow; this they support, by raising innumerable Cavils at the Letter of it, the Diction, the Manner, the Translations, the Difficulties in the Reading, the Inconsistencies, which they call irreconcilable, and the like; by all which they would sink the Divine Authority of it. In a word, they *refuse him that speaketh from Heaven*.[3]

2. They erect a Theologic Phantosm or Apparition, which they call by the Sacred Name of Religion; but very erroneously, and indeed by a direct Forgery. This is called by a new, and, till it was coined for this purpose, an unheard of, Name, *Natural Religion*; which even, when call'd by its right Name, I undertake to prove, is in its plainest and best Construction, neither less or more than *Reveal'd Religion*, and that in its first, and for a while, clearest Revelation.

To this purpose then we shall, in its order, examine what this new Jargon is which these Men speak, and from whence deriv'd; *Natural Light* they acknowlege, *Supernatural Light* they dispise, *Reason* they adore, but *Revelation* they blaspheme: But, let them tell us, is not all Natural Light an Emanation from the Divine? Let them shew us where Nature had any Light at all, and when had Reason any Powers, and from whence? Were they not all from the Author of Nature, which is God? Were they not all given from Heaven, which is Revelation, and nothing else?

But they tell us they will distinguish between Inspiration and Revelation: Very well, let them try their Hands that way: Men are very fond of distinguishing themselves, not into good Principles but out of them,[4] and take much more pains to confound Truth than to explain it: But we are ready to join Issue with them upon that Point also, and to prove the Identity of these Two, as far as Truth is capable of Evidence on Earth.

God having created the Carcase of a Man,[5] for 'tis evident the Body was first form'd, breath'd into him the *Breath of Life*: There was Nature entirely form'd; he receiv'd Life from God; but it does not appear that this Natural Life had any Religious Powers till afterward, when Man became also *a living Soul*,[6] which it is evident was subsequent to his Natural Powers.

Natural Power, which is no more than the sensitive Life, the Locomotive, and other Faculties in common with Brutes,[7] could have no discovery of God, as we see demonstrated too often in the demented Carcase of a Man born an Idiot, inanimate[8] or deprived of the Use of his Reason, which is the Soul; whether by any organnick Impotence, or other occult Defect[9] which Philosophy cannot account for.

Nature then has no Religious Powers, and to say *Natural Religion* is indeed to say nothing, or nothing to the Purpose;[10] 'tis in short to talk Nonsense, a Jargon of Words without Meaning, like the Man of Nature himself without a Soul.[11]

From Nature then, which is thus justly exploded in this Argument, we are led to talk of Reason, and this indeed has something in it to argue from; and were it not a faithful, loyal, and most obedient Subject to its Maker upon all Occasions, acknowleging its Powers to him, and recognizing willingly his just Right to lead and guide it; we might by this time have set it up as a Rebel against God, an Usurper of his Soveraignty, his Providence, and of his Government in the Souls of Men; and, in a Word, made a God of it.

But Reason rejects the offer, and most chearfully bows to its Maker; humble, obsequious, and in a most eminent Manner acknowleging that all its Powers are receiv'd by Inspiration, from the Divine Author of its Being; This Inspiration is upon extraordinary Occasions improv'd, and its Light increas'd by new and glorious Discoveries of God, and of his Will and Works; and this is what we call Revelation.

That there is no room to receive these additional Discoveries and Improvements,[12] and that Reason is at first, and at once, so fully enlightned, that God may not be able to add to its Powers by any subsequent Emanation, is too assuming for us to affirm.

That if there is room to receive them, it should not also be reasonable to do it, would be to set up Reason in the room of God, and erect two infinite perfect Beings in the World; which is blasphemous, and unworthy of God, and, as I said above, is rejected by Reason it self.

What then are these Men doing, while they teach Reason to speak a Language which she understands not, and arm her as a Rebel against her Maker, which she rejects and abhors?

And where will they now (*Archimedes* like)[13] fix their Engine to remove this Globe? Nature is found weak and uncapable, a meer Idiot, a demented inanimate Creature; a Ship without a Rudder,[14] a Chaos truly dark and void; in a word, a Non-Entity as to Religion, having no Knowledge, no Faculties, no Light divine; in a word, no Soul.

As Nature has not the Power, so Reason has not the Will: Nothing acts against itself but it must have a Tendency to its own Destruction. If you will turn Reason to act against, or in the stead of, its Maker, you lead it to destroy itself; all its reasoning Powers center in Almighty Power, and all tend to acknowlege and subject them selves to him.

This is demonstrated in that these reasoning Powers, on all Occasions, confess their own Impotence, and see a Necessity to acknowlege that there are Things yet to be known, which meer reasoning cannot lead us into the discovery of: To say our Reason is sufficient, is to abuse her, and make her say what she knows to be false: Reason's Light must be under some very great and almost total Eclipse, if she does not see a Darkness in herself, when compar'd with that glorious Light that is yet to be reveal'd.

As She sees beyond herself things not to be comprehended by her own Light, and not to be digested by her own Powers; so she earnestly searches into all the Discoveries which her Maker pleases to make to her of things otherwise invisible, and is most humbly obedient *to the heavenly Vision.*[15]

This brief Fundamental destroys at once all the upstart Notions of the Sufficiency of Reason in Matters of Religion: Reason itself bearing Witness to the Reasonableness, and even Necessity, of a further Revelation.

If then all our reasoning Powers are meer Revelations and no more, as is, I think, very clear; and if those very Powers acknowlege their own Defficiency and Imperfection, as they undeniably do, by the insatiable Thirst after farther Knowledge, which all Men find in themselves; then Reason certainly does confess the need she stands in of a farther Discovery, *and that is Revelation.*

As to Nature, or what we so weakly, I might say foolishly, call *Natural Religion,* 'tis quite out of the Question; it seems to have no significancy at all in this Case, any more than it has in itself, which is just nothing at all, unless it may be made use of as the *Igni fatui*[16] of Nature are by Fools to lead them into Bogs and Ditches, Ponds and Rivers, to their Destruction; I shall therefore leave it entirely out of my present Consideration, and if it may be of any use to speak to and expose it farther, shall do so by itself.

We have then no Sceptical Enemy to contend with, but what is thus foolishly grounded;

1. Upon *Natural Light,* which is wholly brutal;[17] and upon the Foot of which a Horse knows as much of God as a Man.

2. Upon the *Light of Reason,* which is in itself Revelation and nothing else; and so is, in the Question before us, in reality nothing at all.

There remains then no more room to contest the Necessity of Revelation. *If Baal be a God let him plead for himself, since Men have thrown down his Altar.*[18] Let then their Modern Deity, which we call REASON, stand up for itself; the Dispute lies in a narrow Compass between Reason and Revelation, as they are now most Sceptically and Deistically understood by the

Free-Thinkers of the Age; and the same Reason and Revelation as they are really in themselves, and as they are seen by their own Light.

If Reason is perfectly enlightned, if it has a self-sufficiency of Knowledge; in a word, if it is infinite in Prescience, and incapable of farther Information, then Reason is GOD;[19] for whatsoever is Infinite is Eternal, *and that is God.*

But whence has Reason all this Illumination? it must be communicated from some prior Being, which is yet more intelligent than Reason itself, or else it could not illuminate it at all.

This prior Being has communicated all the Knowledge it has itself, and then the Thing illuminated is made equal to itself; and so Reason is erected, as before, into an Equality with Infinite, and is set up for a God;[20] or it has not communicated all itself, and consequently there remains yet something farther which may be communicated, *and this is Revelation.*

But granting that God may not have communicated all himself to our Reason, as I shall shew hereafter; they tell us he has reveal'd so much as is sufficient for our use; so much as is necessary to guide us to himself, and to Eternal Felicity, and that is all they plead for. This then brings the Question into still a more narrow Compass than before, for it remains only for them who affirm this, to prove it, and the Question is short. How does it appear that the Lights already given, or reveal'd to our Reason, are sufficient to our Eternal Felicity, and that there is no need of any farther Illumination, or, in a word, that our Reason is perfect in Divine Knowledge?

If indeed this great Affirmative can be proved, they may be said to have gain'd a Point, and all the Discoveries of God in the Scripture, whether of the Old Testament or the New, are of no more Importance in the Case.

But whether will they go[21] for Witnesses, for we must not be put off with Cavils; things will not be demonstrated by Words: Here must be strong Evidence, and where will they find it?

Reason is a Party, and cannot be brought for a Witness on their side: Besides, Reason is against them, as we shall see presently; Scripture also is a Party; whether then will they fly?[22] God and Man being thus directly against them. God and Man, I say, are against them; that is to say, Scripture and Reason: The Scripture is loudly against them, and if Reason were admitted to speak, it would witness against them also. I explain my self thus:

REASON *is against them*; for Reason openly confesses herself not fully enlightned; this she does I say openly, by her constant assiduous Endeavours and unwearied Application after farther Illumination: *Reason* directs us openly to an incessant Search after Knowledge; this I must take for a certain sign that she is sensible of her present Defficiency: It is the strongest Reasoning of its Kind in the World: That Reason is sensible of the Defficiency of her Powers, by her prompting the Minds of Men to encrease in Knowledge, and especially by her frequent Mistakes in the Pursuit of it. See my Lord *Rochester* upon this Subject in his Satyr upon Man.

> *Reason which fifty times for one does err!*[23]

If Reason was sufficiently illuminated, there would be no Mistakes committed by Men in following her Dictates; as if she was perfect in Knowledge, she would be a God; so, if she was sufficiently enlightned in the Case before us, I mean in Religion, she would be an infallible Guide. The contrary to both which we see most true, and that in frequent Examples.

So that Reason, which is the only Evidence the Deists and Free-Thinkers have to bring, to confirm their Sufficiency in Matters of Religion without Divine Revelation, is not only taken from them, and her Evidence made of no effect to their Cause; but she is confronted, and brought against them as a Witness for God, which they can never stand against or resist.

Reason acknowleges she derives from above; 'tis her Glory that she is Heaven born, and came down from God when he caused Man to become *a living Soul*, Gen. ii.7. But she no where pretends to a Perfection of Knowledge, or a Sufficiency of Light; but if she is askt, will, with all humility, say, in the Language of the Text, *it is not in me.*[24]

If God is the Father and Author of our Reason, as doubtless he was, did he give it an Independence of Powers, so that the reasoning Creature had no more occasion of his Maker; or did he place it in a Condition to be continually looking up to its Maker for farther Supplies? The first is an Absurdity in itself, and would place the created Power above the Power creating, which is inconsistent with the Nature of the thing: But if God left this Creature, call'd Reason, in, and under a constant Subservience to, and Dependance upon himself for farther Lights; then God reserv'd it in himself to supply his craving Creature with such farther Emanations, and such other Degrees of Light, as should, upon any subsequent Occasions, be necessary to him; *and this is Revelation.*

Now this Revelation is necessary, or it is not necessary; if it is necessary, then our Reason is not sufficiently enlightned; and if it is not necessary, why does Reason her self search after, rejoice in, and depend upon, farther and more Illuminations? why do we so eagerly desire to know? why enquire daily after what we know not?

Certainly Reason is no infallible Guide in Religion: How many great Men have we seen endowed with the utmost Perfection of human Knowledge; yet groveling in the Dark, and producing the most monstrous Errors, and even Absurdities in the sublimest Parts of Science, and such as are best fitted for Contemplation? an undoubted Evidence that Reason is no perfect Rule, no infallible Judge in Religious things, seeing it is not even in Philosophy itself.

How then do we pretend to lead People from a written Word, in which the Mind and Will of their Creator is revealed, and refer them to that fallible erroneous guiding of the Creature Reason? a Creature who has no Lights of her own, but what are deriv'd to her from the same Fountain of Light from whence all Divine Knowledge is revealed?

And how then do we pretend in Religious matters to depart from the Revelation of Gospel Light, and go back to that of *Reason?* which is itself nothing more or less than a Revelation, and differing only in this sad Circumstance; namely, that it is less clear, less perfect, and less intelligible; for doubtless in all Revelation the subsequent Light is the clearest, the last being an Explanation and Compleating of the former; it is therefore requisite that it should be the most explicit, and fruitful in discovery of Things not fully reveal'd before.

Our Reason is frequently call'd an Emanation of Divine Light,[25] and those People who are now idolizing it among us, frequently compliment Reason with this Title; but then the very same Reason dictates to us, that the Thing deriv'd is less than the Thing deriv'd from; that the Being created is less than the Power creating; and therefore at the same time our Reason bows her Head, and pays Homage to her Creator, confessing that she knows but in part,[26] and that she stands in need of farther Communications of Light and Knowledge from the great Fountain of Wisdom and Knowledge, *and this is Revelation.*

If Reason guides us to look up to him from whose Light she receiv'd all her Lights, what are we doing who take upon us to direct People to look down from him who gave to Reason all her Powers, to that Reason who receiv'd them? as if Reason had receiv'd all that God had to bestow, and that Heaven could add nothing to her former Illuminations?

Again, as Reason acknowleges to have receiv'd all her Powers from God, and looks up continually to him for a farther Emanation; so Reason most readily acknowleges it to be very just, that we should believe whatever the God of Truth shall please to reveal farther to us; for as, if the Scripture is proved to be the Word of God, it is highly reasonable that we should believe it; so if God is pleased to reveal any thing of himself to our Reason, which it was not capable of receiving before, nay, which it may not be capable of comprehending now, Reason agrees readily that it is just we should believe it; because God being himself essential Truth, ought to be believed upon his Word; and Reason submits that he who form'd the Power of Reasoning, and limited it by his Power, may justly be supposed to have yet glorious Truths to reveal, which tho' plac'd out of reach of her present Powers, yet it is reasonable for her to submit herself to, and to believe, because they are his who is the God of Truth and cannot lye.[27]

It is also another Act of just Reasoning, that those Things which Reason itself cannot now comprehend, may yet be reasonably believ'd, and ought to be resign'd to, if they proceed from the Sovereign Hand and God of Truth; seeing it does not follow but that they may be capable of being comprehended even by our Reason itself, when farther enlightned, tho' at present they may seem inscrutable and not to be conceiv'd of.

Thus *Nicodemus*, when the New Birth was describ'd to him by our Saviour, stood at Gaze, and, as may be suppos'd, in a posture of Admiration, expressing himself thus, *How can these things be!*[28] and thus also the Disciples themselves understood not many things which Christ himself had said to them, till afterward, at his Ascension 'tis said, *Then open'd he their understandings, that they might understand the Scriptures*, Luke xxiv. 45[a].

Reason waits at the Foot of her Maker to have her Understanding opened, that she may understand such farther Revelation as he shall please to make to her of himself; and with all possible Reverence submits to believe even all those Revelations he has already made, tho' not at present fully comprehended by her.

N.B. Tho' Scripture is not allow'd in Evidence, while we are arguing with those People, yet we may bring Allusions from Scripture History,[29] as in the Case above, I shall establish the Authority of Scripture in its order, so as not to fear its being exploded by the Cavils of those Men on any Account whatsoever.

Thus far, in general, may serve as an Introduction to this great Truth, That there is a Necessity of Revelation.

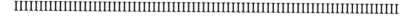

CHAP. II.

That there is no Divine Knowledge among Men, but what began in Revelation, and that all that call'd Natural Religion is a Delusion, an Invention of Man, or rather of the Devil; for that Nature has no Knowledge of Religion, or of Divine Things.

IT is a Maxim in Philosophy, That meer Matter cannot act upon immaterial Objects.[30] We have the same Maxim improv'd in Religious Things, (*viz.*) *That the Natural Man cannot comprehend the things of God;*[31] the Reason of which, is added in the same Text, for they are spiritually discerned.

It is true, that by the Natural Man there, is meant the Unregenerate or Carnal Man, speaking in the Scripture Stile, yet the Metaphor is good still; Nature and Religion are Flesh and Spirit, and I as much wonder to see a Man of Learning, an Author of Fame, tell us of *the Religion of Nature*,[32] as I should have done to have seen a Mathematical description of Nothing: He might as well have delineated the Religion of a Horse: For, as I have said, the Light of Nature is Sense and no more, and informs the Man no more than the sensitive Powers inform a Brute.

Let us therefore talk this Language no more, and, banishing the foolish Expression from our Speech, bring it to what even the People who have made use of this Impropriety, would have us to understand by it, (*viz.*) The Light of Reason.

Another Impropriety I meet with, and which I must take notice of is, That when the Term *Natural Religion* shocks them, as it must do when they come to think of it, they tell us then of *Natural Reason*, which by the way is almost as absurd as the other, and more so as they make use of it in a Religious manner, (*viz.*) setting up this new invented Nothing in the room of Religion.

What can be more inconsistent than the Identity of Nature and Reason? whereas one denominates[33] and distinguishes the brutal and sensitive Life,[34] and the other the rational and superior Life: Natural Religion is an Absurdity in Divinity, and Natural Reason is the same in Philosophy; nor is this Observation useless, much less needless in the Case before us; but far from deserving the Name of a Cavil, it is an essential Objection against all the Religious Schemes of the Infidels of this Age, and overthrows two thirds of their whole Fabrick; for if Nature and Natural be first taken out of their Plea, the whole remaining part will stand upon a very tottering Foundation.

I must therefore be allowed to repeat so much of what is advanc'd in the former Chapter, for establishing the Foundation I am to lay, namely, that all Religion is a Revelation.

I suppose I am not here to dispute Principles; we all agree, That Man is a created Being, he, *that is* God, formed Man of the Dust of the Ground.[35]

His Creation, as a Form or Body, was first in order of Time, it must necessarily be so; for he must be, before he could receive any addition to his Being.

His Form being created, by the same Author of Being he then receiv'd Life, and with that Life a Soul: This Soul receiv'd Powers, or Faculties, call them as we please; these Powers consisted of Understanding and Will; the first contain'd a Fund of Reveal'd Knowledge, with Powers of judging, that is reasoning and determining of its proper Objects, as well superior as inferior, and the last contain'd a directing Power of Action.

All the Light which the Man was made capable of, came in at this Door, from the Knowlege of ordinary Objects, to the Knowlege of the most sublime: By these Powers he was capable of acting upon immaterial Objects, which as a Form, or meer Being, he was not: By these Powers he was made capable of reflecting, ruminating, judging, and understanding Things without, and above, himself; capable of acting upon Futurity, and upon Spirit, in a very extraordinary manner.[36]

Nature had no manner of Concern in this, other than her organick Powers might be made subservient; the Soul having an arbitrary and absolute Dominion in acting by their concurrence and assistance in things only reserv'd to their Operations.

As Nature had no Powers in the ordinary Operations of Life, till animated by the Soul, but was a meer Carcase; much less can it have superiour Powers, which may be so much as named with the Subject we are upon: It is therefore the greatest Absurdity in the World to talk of *Natural Religion*, and it would sound as well to say a Religious Horse, or a Religious Bull, as a Religious Man, demented and stript of his Soul, suppose it were by Idiotism, Disaster, or any organick Defect.

It is wonderful, that in this knowing Age, this vulgar Error should take such footing among us, as to be taught in our Schools, and that the just Distinction should not as readily force its way into our Thoughts, as the gross way of talking on the other side; which must be shocking, and unsonorous[37] to the Ears of Men of Judgment.

To talk of *Natural Religion*, and *Natural Reason!* they are such Inconsistencies, in and with themselves, that it is surprising how Men of Parts and Learning can Account for them; for tho' it may be suggested that we know what they mean, and that they mean nothing but the *Religion of Reason*, and the reasoning Powers in Matters of Religion just as we do; yet, I must say, it is generally expected that Men of right reasoning should argue always in Propriety, and not make use of incongruous Terms, that they may not lay themselves open to such material Reflections, and be at least charg'd with talking unintelligibly.

Nor will it be sufficient to those Men to say, they mean nothing, but, as above, the reasoning Powers of Man, as they are given him with his Life, and are therefore called, with a general Acceptation, by the word *Natural*; for as there is an essential Difference between the sensative Life, and the rational Life in the Man, so there must be observed in all the Discourses upon that Subject, a clear Distinction, and it must run thro' all the Arguments which are made use of upon the same Head; whereas on the contrary, this Absurdity runs through all their Arguments, and through all their Discourses; nor is that all, but in all those Discourses they talk of *Nature*, and the *Religion of Nature*, as if all Religion was really the result of meer Natural Powers, and that Man would have form'd Ideas of God and Religion in his Mind, whether God had added to him a living Soul or no.

Nature is delineated as if it had itself been a free Agent, capable of knowing, and of adoring the Being that made it; and as if the share of such Powers which it had, was such as to be sufficient to its future Happiness, and that Reason and the Soul had no Concern in it. 'Tis true, they do not say so in words at length; but the whole Tenour of their Discourses strongly imply so much, and their Scholars and Pupils are ignorant enough to *speak it out, not knowing*[38] how to distinguish themselves out of the Absurdity, how gross soever it be. And this it is which makes the Observation necessary at this time.

From the Term Natural Religion, as I said above, we are brought on to another Absurdity, almost as gross as the first, and that is *Natural Reason*, an impropriety of the same kind: If it should, in behalf of the Senses of those Men, be insisted on that they do no where use these Terms, and so the Fact[a] should be deny'd, I think I ought to bring some Evidence of the Fact in view, to anticipate such an Objection; and tho' I might, for this purpose, quote the very Term from several Authors who set up to defend the Thing itself, I chuse to take it from an unquestion'd Authority, where the Thing is charg'd upon them in Fact, without any addenda of Observations upon it as an Impropriety; this is from the Second Pastoral Letter of my Lord Bishop of *London*, to the People of his Diocese, publish'd just at the writing these Sheets:[39] His Lordship's Words are these;

> The Infidels of this Age (says my Lord) are endeavouring to lead Men into a disregard of all Revelation, by magnifying the Strength of NATURAL REASON.

It is true, as above, that his Lordship does not animadvert upon the Impropriety of joining the Word, or Epithet, *Natural* to the Term *Reason*; but it is to be observ'd, to the Credit of his Lordship's politer Language, that in his Answer to this Objection, as stated by them, he all along speaks of *Reason*, abstracted from the Word *Nature*, and taking notice of the Thing as it really is, an establish'd Power of thinking, and of judging of Religious Objects, but with no relation to the Powers of meer indigested Nature;[a] he goes on to argue against their corrupt Usage of the Thing, with a strength of reasoning peculiar to himself.

This demonstrates, that with Men of Learning and Judgment, the Distinction is just; and I think, if right speaking be regarded, we shall not hear much more of their Natural Religion, or Natural Reason, the Religion of Nature, and the like.

We are then to bring it all down to its proper Original, which is *Reason*; this they would set up now against Divine Revelation, and insist, that this Reason is fully and sufficiently illuminated, and is the best, and most infallible, Guide in all Religious Cases: So that, in a word, there is no need for us to look any farther, and that all Inspiration, and all Knowlege of Divine things by immediate Revelation, is wholly needless, obsolete, and of no import at all in our inquiry after Heaven.

But we shall find upon inquiry, that they have led themselves into as gross an Absurdity this way as the other; and that Reason's self-sufficiency is a piece of mock Philosophy, that has nothing regular in it; for that, however great this sufficiency of Reason may be in itself, 'tis yet not at all from itself; but is all Exotic, receiv'd from a superior Hand, from a Power without herself,[40] influencing and furnishing all her Faculties; and this I insist is Revelation, and nothing else.

Reason, says an old fashion'd Writer, is God's Candle in the Soul of Man;[41] but that very Notion leads us immediately to ask, who first lighted that Candle, and whose Fire at this time illuminates it? Whence did it receive its first Light? And how came it by a capacity to receive farther Illuminations? Reason's Light, indeed, is antient, for 'tis as old as the first Breath by which *Man became a living Soul*; but this does not authorise us to say, or to suggest, that it is older than Revelation; but that it was really itself a Revelation: As it stood at first upon that Foot, it stands still upon the same Foot, and we have only to inquire, as is said above, whether that first Revelation was full and sufficient to Man, to make himself be his own infallible Guide? an Inquiry, which will afford us an abundant variety of Speculations, all very useful in their Places, and of which we shall have room to speak at large as we go on: In the mean time, it will cause us to give an assent in part to the Letter of what a late Author has publish'd, tho' perhaps not at all in the Sense he design'd it, (*viz.*) That Christianity is as old as the Creation; seeing Christ was reveal'd to the Reasoning Powers, tho' not to the Natural Powers, even of *Adam* in Paradise, and was immediately promis'd as a Redeemer as soon as *Adam* had fallen into Crime.

And this very Thing supports, not the Justice only, but the Force of the Distinction I make between the Religion of our Reason, and that unsignifying Thing,[42] call'd, the Religion of Nature; for, it is not a Distinction without a Difference; the Infidels we are to talk with, have made the Distinction just; for this Religion of Nature, and this Natural Reason, they would make a kind of Light which Man is master of, by they know not what independant Power, as a Consequence of his being, not as a Gift from the Bounty of his Maker; whereas Man's reasoning Powers are all eminently deriv'd from the Divine Benevolence, bestow'd in a supernatural way, namely by Emanation; they have also a tendency to Loyalty and Obedience to that God from whom they do proceed, and upon all Occasions recognize the Power bestowing them, looking up to him for the continuance and encrease of his Gifts, and this will necessarily be the Subject of the next Chapter.

IIIIIIIIIIIIIIIIIIIIIIIIIIIIIIIIIIIIIIIIIIIIIIIIIIIIIIIIIIIIIIIIIIIIIIIIIIIIIIIIIIII

CHAP. III.

*That Reason itself is a Beam of Divine Light, issuing from God himself,
inspir'd at first with the Soul of Man, and continu'd since by additional
Inspirations from the same Power, which first, as well as all the subsequent
Inspirations from Heaven, by which his Soul is farther inlightned, is nothing
more, or less, than a Divine Revelation.*

INSPIRATION and Revelation, are so far Synonimous Terms, that the Difference seems to lie not in the Thing, so much, as in the common Acceptation of the Terms, which have been understood thus, (*viz.*) That Inspiration seemed to regard the ancient Prophets, and the manner how God inspir'd them from Heaven with a Spirit of Prophesy, for foretelling things to come, and these were call'd inspir'd Men, and Men of God, as likewise the Apostles, and first Fathers of Christianity, who were inspir'd with the Holy Ghost.

Revelation seem'd to regard the Matter which they were inspir'd with, which was afterwards made the Subject of their teachings and preaching to the World, in which they are said to declare the Mind and Will of God to Men, as well in particular, as in general Instructions, Warnings, Exhortations, and the like.

But abating this publick or common Acceptation of the Words, we shall find they all issued in the same Thing; namely, a Revelation of the Mind and Will of God to Men.

I believe no Man will contend, that God did not reveal himself, and his Mind, and Will, to the first created Man, over and above all the first inspir'd Gifts with which his Soul was endow'd: I doubt not but the Soul, with all its Endowments, was as compleat in *Adam*, as I believe was ever communicated to any of his Posterity, even to this Day; and yet we find several farther Revelations of the Mind and Will of God made to him in Paradise, and perhaps afterwards,[43] all which we must suggest were needless and impertinent; or we must allow that the first Revelation, or Inspiration of his Reason, was not intended to be sufficient.

If *Adam* had a fully inspir'd Soul, what need was there of a reveal'd Law? what need farther Commands to be laid upon him? his Original Lights were as sufficient Guides as any Man has come into the World with since; for they were all from God, and that immediately by Inspiration, which is the same thing as Revelation; yet 'tis apparent, that his Inspiration was but a partial Degree of Knowledge in divine Things, and that he was to receive farther and farther Discoveries of God by the same Hand, and by the same Manner, namely, by Revelation.

If then all the Knowlege, which the Soul of Man was at first inspir'd with, was a Divine Revelation, how do we come to distinguish ourselves into new Notions of the Original of that Knowlege, as if it came some other way? The reasoning Powers are all from God, all breathed into Man with his *Soul,* all Divine Knowlege, and the Power to use it and encrease it, was thus *reveal'd* to him, and all the Addenda of that Knowlege are by the same Method; namely, by *a farther Revelation.*

The Force of this way of arguing shews itself to be undeniable; because as it is impossible the Nature of the Man should receive any Impressions of Religion at all; so it is equally impossible the Soul of Man should receive them by any other way, than as a Revelation from that supreme Being, from whence, alone, all Divine Knowlege must derive.

This the Author of that monstrous Mass of Absurdity, call'd *Christianity as old as the Creation,* is oblig'd to come into, at his very first launching upon the Ocean of Error, which we see him plung'd into, *Page* 3. his Words are these: "*Natural Religion* differs not from *Reveal'd,* but in the Manner of its being communicated, *the one* being the Internal, and the other the External Revelation."

And what is this now but *Inspiration* and *Revelation,* which as I observ'd above, are one and the same Thing? And how are the worst Infidels, by the meer Necessity of their own reasoning, however wickedly design'd, brought to recognize the very Thing they would explode: But, to evade the Consequences of it, they at the same time, commit a second Error, worse than the first; namely, they insist that the first Revelation is perfect, and that all farther *Revelation* is needless and impertinent; by which they impeach the Wisdom of God for giving, what they call, an imperfect Revelation at first, or confine and restrain the Almighty from giving out any farther discoveries of his Mind and Will to Mankind, than what he at first thought fit to communicate to him; all which are arrogant and assuming[44] in the highest Degree.

For the first, we grant, that it was a most righteous and perfect Law which God gave to Man, at the time that he gave him a living Soul; it was certainly a Revelation of so much of his Mind and Will, as was sufficient to his eternal Felicity, and to all that God required of him, at that time: But 'tis as certain, that there were many things, which were needful to be discover'd to him after his Fall, which he was not able to have known, or comprehended before: If not, then *Adam* had a certain full understanding in his Soul, of the universal will of God, both relating to his present, and his subsequent Circumstance of Life, the very Moment he became a living Soul; which, as it is not reasonable to believe, so it is impossible to prove.

It was enough that *Adam* had an immediate Knowlege of every thing which God, his Maker, thought needful for him to know at that time; and sufficient, if he had pursued it, to have directed him to a perfect Obedience to God's Law: Besides which, he had a capacity of Soul to receive such farther degrees of Knowlege by Revelation, or otherwise, as his Maker should see needful to communicate; nor is it any Impeachment of the Wisdom or Goodness of his said Maker, that he might thus reserve in himself the Right, as well as the Power, of such farther Revelation, and the Knowlege of things to be communicated, when, and in what manner he thought fit; and this makes it not only clear that the Redemption of Mankind by Christ, the *Messiah*, was first promised in the beginning of Time; but that it was afterwards perform'd and brought forth in the fulness of Time,[45] according to, and in pursuance of, that Promise; otherwise, because God would not have given an imperfect Law, he must upon *Adam*'s Fall, have immediately sent his Son into Paradise to have restored *Adam*; it might as well be said, he might have actually made *Adam* perform a perfect Obedience to his Law, and so have prevented any falling at all; all which, it would be the utmost Arrogance as well as Impiety, to say ought to have been done; and it is most certain it was not done; because *Adam* fell from his first rectitude of Soul, in which 'tis evident, that tho' he had a capacity to Obey, yet he was not under a force compelling him to Obey.

I know some of these Men deny any such thing as a Fall; they are forced to it by their way of Reasoning; but the propensity in the Will of Man to offend, and to break continually with his Maker (which appears to this Day, and which they dare not deny) evinces the Fact, (*viz.*) that *Adam* fell, the Evidence is so strong, that their own Scheme is full of it; for while they affirm, that Man has a Power in his Soul, namely, his Reason, to perform a sincere, and what they call a perfect Obedience, they yet grant, that he does not do it, but often fails, transgresses, turns Rebel, and offends against God.

Now, why is it not as much an Impeachment of the Wisdom and Goodness of a righteous God, that he did not put Man not only into a Capacity, but under the Force and Necessity of compleat Obedience; as it is that he did not make a full and compleat Revelation to him of all that should ever be necessary for him to do or to know? And this I think may be a full Answer to all the Cavils of those who exalt their Phantosme,[46] call'd *Natural Religion*, in the room of the ordinary course of God's Methods with Mankind, for his farther and daily Direction in his way to Heaven.

But this leads me too far out of my way, I return therefore to the Subject of this present Chapter; namely, that the first Knowlege of God in the Mind, and to the Will of Man, was all by Revelation, and that all subsequent Revelation is no more than an Appendix to those first Lights.

The first gift God gave, to his yet unfinish'd Creature, was *a Soul*. This Soul either consisted of innate Qualities, as some will have it, such as we call Capacities, Faculties, and Powers; or was a Vessel only, made capable of receiving such Powers as his Maker should from time to time see fit to give. Some of his Powers were, without doubt, bestow'd at first, and seem to be the constituent parts of a Soul. But certainly those Powers were capable of receiving new Lights, an Encrease of Knowlege, and farther Discoveries from his Maker every Day, as God should please to communicate himself to him.

I think this demonstrable, even from the Additions which we every Day receive in human, as well as Divine Things; whether they are communicated in a way of Providence, or of superior Discovery, is not material; we see they are really communicated, and we see our Reason is not only aspiring after higher Illuminations, but is every Day obtaining them: To say every Man may pursue the highest and most perfect Dictates of Reason, as God has given this Reason for a perfect Rule, is contradicted, even by our Experience, in that all Men are not alike qualify'd to make use of the Reason which they are possess'd of; the actings of the Soul are in some prescrib'd, and narrow'd[47] by one accident, and in others by a distorting Cause; here the Organ is defective, there the Powers are narrowed; will these be justify'd before God, for the imperfect use of that Degree of Reason which they had? and yet is the sincere use of that Reason, the grand Defence that we may make for all our Imperfections.

I am very ready to acknowlege, the free and unprejudic'd use of Reason, to be a very great step in our way to Heaven; but I can by no means grant that it is a sufficient Rule, and that if it be adher'd to so far as we say we can adhere to it, *it justifies us before God*; and that *God cannot in justice require any more of us*:[48] 'Tis a way of talking that we have not been used to; it may be true, that every Offender, at the same time that he offends God, sins also against his own Reason; but it cannot be true that this is all his guilt.

But I would fain know how this obeying the Voice of Reason comes to be called Christianity, I readily allow that Christianity is as old as the Fall of Man, that is, not far off of the Creation; but how comes this Religion, which they call *the Religion of Reason*, to be thus *nick-nam'd* Christianity; we all know that in the common Acceptation, the meaning of the word Christianity is the Profession of Faith in the MESSIAH, *which is, being interpreted*, the CHRIST;[49] and that Believers in Christ are called Christians, and have been so from the first Church of New Converts, erected at *Antioch.*[50] But how comes our modern Infidels, who expect to be justify'd by the meer use of their Reason, and that *this is all God can demand of them*; I say, How can they prophane the sacred Name of Christ, and the Religion of the *Holy Jesus*, by guilding their Idol with it in such a manner, and set up their infallibility of Reason, which is itself a dark and dirty, and many ways a fallible instrument, and call it Christianity?

The just Remarks upon this gross Absurdity might well pass, even by itself, for a full Answer to his whole *Volume.* To call his Light of Reason a Gospel, and his new modelled Principle of obeying Reason, Christianity, is to me so inconsistent with the Doctrine of Christ, that nothing can be more contrary to it.

To say God has given Man no other Faculties to judge with, but those by which we are distinguish'd from Brutes, is to say, that the Christian has no other Power to judge by than a Heathen, and perhaps, in the literal Sense of the word, it may be true; because, as he says, we are ordered to *examine the Truth of all the Gospel Revelation:*[51] But to add that the Christian has not those Faculties farther illuminated, and his Soul led into a higher and different Exercise, by the help of farther communicated Lights from above, is to cast off all Christianity at once; by which we are made to hope for the Assistance and secret Influences of the Blessed Spirit of Truth, who shall *guide us into all Truth,*[52] shall *teach us all things*, and *bring all things to our remembrance.*[53] This, I say, is Christianity; now as they reject this Spirit, call it an Enthusiasm, make it the Subject of their Ridicule, and tell us that using the reasonable Faculties after the best manner we can, must *justify us before God*, and at the same time talk of Christianity, I say they are guilty of the most monstrous Absurdity.

The Knowlege of a God is the first Introduction to all Religion; for the being of a God being recogniz'd by his rational Creature, the worshiping (that is paying a Homage to) that God is an irresistable consequence; Reason directs, Reason commands it; but all the Light of Reason in the politest of Men, could never direct the manner by which God was pleas'd to accept of his Creatures Homage, till God himself was pleased to direct it by a farther Illumination, which, in a word is Revelation and nothing else;[54] as is excellently well observ'd in the Bishop of *London*'s second Pastoral Letter, mentioned above, and publish'd on this very Occasion.

Nor do I see, as these Men pretend they do, the Necessity there was that God should communicate his whole Will to the first Branches of the human Race; what he thought fit to communicate to them, might be so far his whole Mind and Will to them, as that it was their perfect rule to walk by, which if they had perfectly obey'd, there seems to be no room to doubt, they would have been accepted.

God himself, speaking to *Cain*, tells him so much, thus (*viz.*) *If thou doest well, shall thou not be accepted?*[55] This doing well consisted in acting according to the Revelation then made: But certainly there are things required of us since that time, which would not have been possible for *Cain* to have perform'd, and therefore God did not require them; but as the Will and Commands of God are extended to a farther Degree than they were then, so Man has farther Powers of Obedience given to him, other Duties commanded, and farther means of knowing and obeying them communicated; and this by the same Method of Revelation.

And why should it not be as just with God, in different lengths and periods of Time, to require other acts of Obedience from Man, than he at first gave him the Knowlege of, and the Power to perform? and this upon giving additional Powers, both to know and to obey, as it is to require that the Earth should not bring forth Fruits, and Products once Natural to it, without the future Labour of Man cultivating it, and improving it by Husbandry; and even with that addition, yet not without fructifying Showers, refreshing Dews, and the other half as well of Nature as of Art, and that upon those Applications it should be fruitful. We do not object that it was any Imperfection in God, that his first *Fiat*[56] did not give Man a Law to reach all that was required of him, or should ever be requir'd of any Man after him.

Doubtless the first revelation of the Duty, owing to God by his Creatures, had it been perfectly obey'd, had been sufficient to the Man if he had obey'd it; but he failing in his Obedience, God has thought fit to change his situation, and he stands now upon another foot of Obedience than he did before; and 'tis happy for him that he does so; for, whereas before, nothing but a perfect Obedience could be accepted; now through the Merit and Sacrifice of the *Messiah*, an imputed Righteousness[57] is accepted for him, and he is justify'd in the Merit of a Redeemer.

Was this reveal'd to *Adam* in his perfect State? Certainly it was not, and therefore 'tis a mistake, *to say no worse of it*; to tell us that Christianity is as old as the Creation, which I shall state clearly by itself, *Adam* had a perfect

Law given to him in the State of Innocence; but *Adam* broke with God, and upon that Breach his Affairs took a new Turn *as we call it*,[58] and then came the Gospel Revelation, as we shall see presently.

But to go back to the State of Innocence, all the Religion *Adam* had, and which was planted in him, with his Reason, was a plain and evident Revelation, and nothing else; so that the Religion of Reason is no more or less than this, (*viz.*) A Revelation of the Will of God to the Soul of Man, at the same time, and as soon as God gave him a Soul to receive it.

Let us now grant, and lay it down as an establish'd Principle, that *Adam*, in his State of Innocence, had a perfect inlightned Soul, and a compleat Knowlege and Will of the righteous Law which his Maker had given him; he knew also, that he had a Power to Obey, and his Obedience according to that Knowlege and Power, would, without doubt, have been accepted, if it had been, as it ought to have been, full and compleat.

> *N. B.* These People seem to be placing us now, after so many Ages of Corruption in the very same Station and Circumstance of Life as *Adam* was in his Innocence; namely, that we have a Perfect Law, which if we sincerely live up to, (adding that we have a Power also to live up to it) God will, nay must, accept us; let them stand to that Point, and we shall soon see them plung'd into a Gulph of confus'd Notions, which it is impossible to extricate them out of, but by the Doctrine of a farther Revelation.

If *Adam* had liv'd up to the first Law, which was the Rule of his Obedience, he had remain'd innocent; but *Adam* did not sincerely obey that Law, or follow the Dictates of the reasoning Light, with which God had endow'd him: And pray what was *Adam*'s Case then? His being accepted, was then no more the Question; nothing but the threatn'd Death, which we all have read of, ensued: Could *Adam* have said to God, I have offended indeed, but I will obey exactly for the future, and sincerely walk according to all the means thou hast given me to know, or the Rules thou hast given me to walk by, and therefore such a future Obedience must justify my Conduct, because thou hast not given me any other Lights to walk by.

Would this have been a sufficient Plea for *Adam*, without any Retrospect to the Breach he had made, and the Rebellion he had been guilty of? If it had, then the same Resolution of Amendment will do still, and be sufficient for us all, tho' we break that new Engagement a thousand times a Day; and God is bound to pass by, and take no Notice of, much less resent any of our most horrid Excursions[a59], be it Rapine or Murder, Adultery, Perjury, or any more flagrant Offence: A fine easy way this is of being accepted by our Maker!

But *Adam*'s Affairs stood in another Situation, and so do ours also; for *Adam* having broken that most just and Righteous Law, stood immediately, *as it were* at the Bar of God's Justice, as a Criminal; and had his Trespass to answer for, according as is exprest in Gen. chap. iii. 13. *What is this that thou hast done?* Nor was *Adam* ignorant; sense of guilt immediately struck him; his Reason was strong enough to tell him he had offended, tho' it immediately suffer'd him to act the weakest and most foolish Part that ever any reasonable Creature did; namely, to hide himself among a few Bushes from the Search of, INFINITE![60] and then to cover his Nakedness from the sight of Beasts;[61] was this the Work of a perfectly inlightned Soul? was it not a certain Token of the Weakness of humane Reasoning, and how much it stood in need of farther Illumination?

But to return: *Adam* having offended, how stood the Case between God and him, as to the Law of his Reason, and the Rule of his Life; and what did his self-sufficient Knowlege do for him? and here leaving the Scripture Account,[62] because these Men dispise it: This is certain by the History of the first Times: Their Reason might dictate to them that there was a God, and it did so: And Reason also dictated that he was to be worshiped; all the World came into these Things by the meer reasoning Light.

Nulla gens tam barbara quæ nescit esse Deum.[63]

But how dim and dark was this Light! they neither retain'd right Notions of this God; who, or what he was, or what his Mind and Will was; much less did they entertain the least Notion of the *Modus* of his Worship;[64] how, and in what manner, he would be approach'd, or in what manner, he would now accept of the Homage of his Creatures; and this Ignorance ran thro' the whole Race, the wrong Notions of worshipping God, which these self-sufficient Creatures formed, in their highest reasoning Capacities, fill'd the World with the grossest Idolatries, and the vilest Corruption of things sacred, that could possibly be imagined.

But to *Adam*, and to those few to whom God was pleas'd farther to reveal himself, the Case differ'd: No sooner was the Promise of the *Messiah* (the Seed of the Woman) given to him, but he was immediately taught from Heaven, what it was *God would have him to do*; namely, to return to God by Repentance; to accept of and believe the Promise of a *Messiah*, and to worship, in the sincerest manner, and in the most acceptable way, the supreme *Being*; GOD had, notwithstanding the Sentence of Death pass'd on him, by the righteous first Law which he had broken, mercifully spar'd him from the Death he had deserv'd; and reveal'd a Saviour to his Faith that should heal this Breach between God and him, and make a full satisfaction in his stead, and that by offering an accepted Sacrifice, even that of his own incarnate Body and Blood, as is preach'd in all the process of the Gospel.[65]

This being the Case with *Adam*, we see the Facts immediately acted upon the Stage of Life; *Adam*, a sincere Penitent for his first Offence, applied himself, after his exclusion from Paradise, to Labour, as the Text implies, and brought up his Sons to do the like. Hence we find *Cain*, the eldest Son, and Heir-Apparent to the Empire of the World, was a Plowman; and *Abel* his Brother, a Grasier; *Gen.* iv. 2. *Abel* was *a keeper of sheep,* and *Cain* was *a tiller of the ground.*

Reason might very well dictate to them, that they must apply themselves to such Work; since God had expressly told them upon the Fall, that the Ground, being curs'd for their sake, should bring forth nothing naturally, that is, not without Cultivation, which we call to this day in some Dialects, labouring the Land;[66] and that in the sweat of his Brows[67] he should eat his Bread. All this, I say, *Adam's Reason* might lead him to; but what he was to do towards reconciling himself to God after his sad Fall and Defection from him; and how, or in what manner, to pay his Homage to him in the mean time; of all this *Adam* could know nothing, 'till God reveal'd his merciful Design of a Redemption for him; by his Son, the *Messiah*; and from this *Messiah*, who was to be offer'd up for his sins, with the promises of accepting Sinners on his account, came all the intervening Sacrifices of the Law, and in the practice of which, the Heathen Nations follow'd the Example.

Now whence came this Knowlege of the Mind and Will of God, as to Man's Recovery, and of his Repentance, and Faith in the promis'd Seed? Man knew nothing of it before the Fall; nor in the Guilt and Terror of the Fact did he know any thing of it; he thought of nothing but of running away like a Fool, when he knew not whither to go; and hiding himself, as above, from Omniscience itself. The Light of his Reason, tho' so clear and good, shew'd him nothing of what was his Duty in that unhappy Condition; all this must certainly come by a subsequent Revelation; and therefore Mr. *Milton*, with an admirable Turn of Invention,[68] brings in the Angel as sent from Heaven to inform *Adam* of his State and Condition; how sunk by his Fall, how to be recover'd by his Repentance, and by his Faith in the promis'd Mercy of a *Messiah*; who should offer up an accepted sacrifice to God, as a Propitiation for him, and all his believing Posterity; and how in the mean time, as Types of the great Attonement[69] through the Blood of the *Messiah*, God required a series of other Sacrifices upon the occasion of future Transgressions, whose Blood being offered up, and having a View towards the great Attonement and Sacrifice of Christ, should be accepted of God.

Hence came the Knowlege of true Religion into the World, and that it must be by a glorious Revelation of the Mind and Will of God, for the eternal Salvation of Men, seems out of all question; because, as above, *Adam* himself, by the light of the most exalted Reason, knew nothing at all of it.

Here therefore, as a farther Testimony of the Fact, I demand of these new Religion-makers, how came *Cain* and *Abel* to know that God would be propitiated by a sacrifice? What was the meaning of bringing a Lamb, or firstling as 'tis call'd,[70] of the Flock, and a Basket of Corn, or whatever other Fruits of the Earth it might be, and *burning them to God*.[71] Where was the sense of it, and what could meer Reason say to it? Had they been given personally, and the Lord of Heaven had taken them as a Quit-Rent for the Tenure of the Lands they held,[72] it had been something rational, it had look'd like *a reasonable Service*;[73] but who could instruct them to set them on fire, and that in order to be accepted they must first be destroyed, and yet this was called in *Abel*, at least, an *acceptable Sacrifice*, Heb. xi. 4.[a74]

Was it a rational Homage, or a reveal'd, that an innocent Lamb should first be kill'd, and his Blood pour'd out, and then his Flesh burnt to Ashes, as a Tribute to a righteous and merciful Being, the King of Heaven! and yet this was the Case; it was first done without the help of any reasoning Light, and the whole Pagan World has follow'd the Pattern ever since; 'till believing that God ought to be honour'd with the best sacrifices they could procure, they came at length to offer up their own Children, and give *the Fruit of their Bodies, for the Sin of their Souls*.[75]

But let us keep where we are,[76] and look at it thro' the Glass, or Light, of Reason in its fullest strength: How incongruous was the very thing call'd a Sacrifice, or Burnt-Offering,[77] to the very Notion of Religion, and to the most reasonable Thoughts of the Beneficence of a merciful God! Reason could have no Notion of it; 'twas altogether inconsistent with the first Discoveries of a supreme Being; it must come by an immediate Intelligence with[78] and a subsequent Communication of the Mind and Will of God to Mankind, and this is all Revelation and nothing else.

If then this Revelation, or Discovery of the Mind and Will of God, was subsequent to the perfect Law, which these men pretend was given him at his Creation; then that Law was not compleat at first, and if not compleat at first, then the sincerest Obedience to that first Law cannot be all that God can expect or require of man, as is now advanc'd; for doubtless Heaven would expect the like sincere Regard to be paid to the subsequent Communication, as he did to the first.

IIIIIIIIIIIIIIIIIIIIIIIIIIIIIIIIIIIIIIIIIIIIIIIIIIIIIIIIIIIIIIIIIIIIIIIIIIIIIIIIIIIIIIIIII

CHAP. IV[a].

Of the true Antiquity of CHRISTIANITY, *and that it is not as old as the Creation, tho' very near it; Also of the Absurdity of calling the* Religion of Reason, *in the modern Sense of that Word, by the name of* CHRISTIANITY.

BEING to speak of the Antiquity of *Christianity*, in this Chapter, it is necessary to observe, that the learned Author referr'd to has not, as I think he ought, explained his Terms; or told us what we are to understand by the thing Christianity, having left us to determine of it, every one as he pleases.

I must not fall into the same Error, but must at least give my Explanation of it, not only as I think of it, but as I think we are all unavoidably led by the Tenor of his Discourse, to suppose every one must understand it, and that he understands it so himself.

By *Christianity* therefore, I understand the *Religion of Jesus*; that Religion that leads us to believe in, and rest upon *Jesus Christ* for Life and Salvation, acknowleging him to be the *Life* and *Light* of the World,[79] and that whoever believes in him shall not perish, but have everlasting Life;[80] believing him to be the Way, and the Truth, and the Life, and that no man cometh unto the Father but by him;[81] believing that God promised him in the first Ages of Time, so call'd the *Beginning of Time*;[82] and afterwards sent him in the Fullness of Time, not to condemn the World, but that the World through him might be saved. *John* iii. 17.

The Servants of this *Jesus* were called Christians,[83] and the Doctrine of Faith and Repentance which is preached in his Name, and has been preach'd and profess'd so many Ages is Christianity, and has been always called so.

Having thus explained what I think is generally understood by Christianity, I deny that this Christianity is as old as the Creation; and I make it good by proving the direct contrary Proposition; *namely*,

That there was a Time after the Creation, when Christianity, or the Christian Religion, was not.

When the first Man stood firm in his created perfect state, pure and holy as he came out of the hands of his Creator, his Obedience to his Maker perfect, and his Innocence compleat, when Sin was not entred into the World, nor *Death by Sin*,[84] there was no need of a Saviour, no need of a sacrifice, for *Adam* having no Sin there could be no Expiation; God being not offended, there could be no Propitiation;[85] the Seed of the Woman was not in Promise, much less in Expectation, less still was it an Object of Faith; as there was no Christ wanted, so there was no Christ promised; as there was no Sin, there was no Death, and no Redemption in view; no *Christ*, and consequently no *Christianity*.[86]

How long *Adam* continued in that blessed state of Innocence, Revelation is silent; the written Word has not mentioned it, nor has Tradition suggested any thing towards it; as for the crude Guesses and Pretences of Men about it, they are so absolutely void of Rule, and of Foundation to judge by, that I esteem it the highest Presumption in us to enter into the Enquiry, and as much so in those that adhere to them or to their Guesses as authentic; and therefore I say no more to it but this, whether three days only, or an hundred Years, or how much more or less, the thing (as blessed be God all such Enquiries are) is as needless as it is impossible to know.[87]

But be it more or less, this is certain, and is sufficient to the Argument, that during that whole blessed Interval, between the Creation and the Fall, CHRISTIANITY WAS NOT.

There is a Cavil indeed rais'd against this, and it is no more than a Cavil, and shall be no more than nam'd, (*viz.*) that there was no such Interval at all; but that the two first rational Creatures sinn'd as soon as they were made, that the Soul rebelled even the same Hour that it was breathed into the Body of the Man; that no sooner was the perfect Law of God, the Rule of their Obedience given them, or laid down as a Command, but the soul of the Woman first objected against it as hard and unjust, and resolv'd not to obey it; and that the Man coming into the same sentiments, join'd with her in the Rebellion.

This Cavil I only name, as I promis'd above; because first of all, it is evident, that it cannot be known; and, secondly, that it seems to be highly improbable to be true. But the first is sufficient to silence it in this place, seeing what cannot be known cannot be proved, and ought not to be received as an establish'd Proposition.

That there must be some Interval between the Creation and the Fall, is to me demonstrable, from the several steps necessary for the giving a Law to the Man after he was created, and for expecting his Obedience; and tho' we were to pass from the Account given of it in the Scripture, which yet I do not; yet I say the nature of the thing makes it necessary, that after the Law given to *Adam*, as the Rule of his Conduct, and during his Obedience to which he continued innocent, there must be some space of Time, be it much or little, in which he remain'd obedient and innocent, enjoy'd the Paradise he was plac'd in, and was a compleatly happy Creature; it is not at all likely, that he was created, plac'd in Paradise, receiv'd a Law, transgress'd that Law, was sentenc'd to Death, had the Doctrine of Repentance preach'd to him, and a Christ to redeem him promis'd, and was then turn'd out of the Garden into the wide World, all in the same instant; I say it is not probable, much less demonstrable.

This Interval then, let it be what it will, long or short, a hundred years, or not a year, is the time in which, as above CHRISTIANITY WAS NOT, and therefore it cannot be as old as the Creation.

But having laid this down as a Proposition, which I think is self-evident, I come very readily into the real Antiquity of the Christian Religion, and agree, that the Promise of Christ was the first and immediate Product of the merciful Disposition of God to his Creature (fallen and lapsed as he was) and was promulgated to man as the Object of his Faith immediately after his Fall; and had the Author I mention said in the Title Page of his Book, that Christianity was as old as the sentence pass'd upon the Man after his Fall, he had said right.

But this would not serve to his purpose, for he would by his pretended Antiquity of Christianity represent it to us, as what he calls a natural Principle; which were I to grant his Notion of *Natural* as annex'd to *Religion* would not do; for Christianity was not infus'd with the Soul, it was not an innate Idea,[88] but was evidently a subsequent Revelation; Christ being publish'd to *Adam*, and promised in those Words included in the sentence upon the Serpent, *Gen*. iii. 15. *And I will put enmity between thee and the woman, and between thy seed and her seed: and it shall bruise thy head, and thou shalt bruise his heel.*

This was the Promise of the Messiah, which, according to Scripture Interpretation, is the Christ, *Joh*. I. 41. *We have found the Messiah, which is, being interpreted, the Christ.*

The Faith of this Promise, that is to say believing in this *MESSIAH* who was to come, and of whom *Philip* said to *Nathanael*, *Moses* in the Law, and the Prophets, did write; see the same first of *John* ver. 45. I say this Faith was really Christianity (tho' it was not call'd by that Name) as much as Faith in the same Christ is now after he is already come.

That the Patriarchs did thus understand it, and that all the faithful did thus believe, is evident in sacred History, in abundance of Places, and tho' it is not called by the Name Christianity, as we now express it, yet 'tis plain to be read tho' in other Expressions, such as that of *Jacob*, when he was blessing his Sons, *Gen.* xlix. 18. *I have waited for thy Salvation, O Lord*; the meaning whereof is no more or less than this, I have believed thy Promise of a Christ to be the Salvation of thy People. In another place he is called the Consolation of *Israel*, Luke ii. 25. *Simeon* was just and devout, *waiting for the Consolation of Israel*. In the same Chapter, *ver.* 38. 'tis said that *Anna*, the Prophetess, *spake of Jesus to all them, that looked for redemption in* Jerusalem. Again, it is said of *Joseph* of *Arimathea,* Luke xxiii. 51. *That he waited for the Kingdom of God.*

All these Texts being Historical, may, as I said before, be referr'd to in proofs of Fact, namely, to prove that the Jews, such of them, as were just and devout, believ'd in, and waited for the Salvation of the Jews, by the coming of the promis'd Seed, of which all the Books of the Old Testament were full, and it was generally called by those exalted Titles, the Salvation of God, the Redemption of *Israel*, the Salvation of *Israel*, the Kingdom of God, and the like. And what is this, in short, but the Promise of Salvation by a Redeemer to be sent, and this Redeemer being Christ, and no other, what is all this but Christianity?

So that thus the Christian Religion has been evidently professed by all true Believers, ever since the Promise made of a Seed which should break the Head of the Serpent; and that was immediately after the Fall of Man.[89]

Mr. *Calvin,* in his Institutions,[90] gives us one whole and large Discourse, speaking of the Redemption of Man since his Fall, by a Saviour, to expound to us all the Prophets, and in all the Places where they so evidently speak of and predict the coming of Christ into the World to redeem his Church, and this he does with so much Clearness, that it seems to admit of no Controversy, that in all the Ages of the Mosaic Dispensation, the Eyes of all the Believing Jews were guided, even by every Sacrifice and every Ceremony of the whole Law, to look forward to, and wait for, Christ as the Salvation and Redemption of his People, and what is this but Christianity?

Thus, as soon as Man sinn'd against his Maker, the Mercy of God, interposing, establish'd a Saviour, which is called therefore the Salvation, and the Consolation of *Israel*;[91] him *Adam* himself saw, and believ'd him that had promis'd; and we see the Author of that glorious Epistle to the Hebrews, commenting upon this antient Faith thus, Heb. xi. 13. *These all died in Faith, not having receiv'd the Promises,* that is not having seen them fulfill'd by the coming of the Messiah; but he adds, *Having seen them afar off, and being perswaded of them, and embrac'd them*: This confirms it past all doubt, that the Fathers, (so the same Author to the Hebrews calls them) before Christ, believed in Christ, were perswaded of, and embraced the Promises of Christ, tho' he was seen only as at the greatest imaginable distance of Time.

All this is in Proof of the Antiquity of Christianity, or of the Christian Faith; but it is plain also, that this confirms what I have said above, that before *Adam* had sinn'd, Christianity was not: While he had not fallen, what need was there of his being lifted up? What need of a Saviour to restore him, a Sacrifice to attone for him? Christ was not heard of, or the Promise of a Seed made; neither was it of any moment to *Adam* (unless it had been reveal'd to him, that he would certainly fall, break with his Maker, and rebel against God) if that had been known to him, indeed, it might be probable; but there was no likelihood of any such thing, the very suggestion of it is preposterous, and we may as well suggest that he would not have fallen if it had been fore-told him; which, however, is all remote from the present Question.

But what does all this amount to? I answer, It fully proves to us, that this Gospel Dispensation, was not an Original planted in the Soul of Man, at its being first breathed into his Body, which is the very thing we have pro-posed; that it was not twisted in with his Reason, and form'd with him in such a manner, as that he could not exercise his Reason without it, as the first general Notions of a God are: But that it is all a meer Revelation, a dis-covery made to him subsequent to his Offence; a merciful appointment of Grace and Mercy to him, when he was as it were sunk in the utmost depth of Misery and Distress, under the Weight of a threatned Curse; to talk of this before his Fall, would be to the last degree absurd, for what need of saving that which was not lost?

Hence, I say, it is evident that the Promise of Christ was subsequent to the Fall of Man, and not heard of before it; and hence during all the Interval between the Creation, and the Fall CHRISTIANITY WAS NOT; and when IT WAS, when it had a Being in the Promise of Christ, it was all a Revelation, and all subsequent to the first Inspiration, or Revelation of Religion to the Soul of Man.

What then can the Patrons of the Religion of Reason, or of Nature, let them call it by what gross Terms they please, I say, what can they gain by trac-ing back the Religion of [a] *Jesus*, which they call Christianity, to the Fall of Man? Indeed they can get nothing by it, but to bring out the clearest Evidence of its being at first all Revelation, a Religion unknown to Man in his Original State, utterly conceal'd from him, and not discover'd till made necessary, by his Misery, to support his Soul under the Weight of his Sorrows, bring him to true Repentance, and show him a way of Salvation, which all the Light of his Reason could see nothing of.

Thus they have been made the Underminers of their own Cause, and have rais'd Arguments against themselves, even out of their own Objection.

And to confirm this yet farther, here is an evident Proof, that the making a subsequent Revelation to Man, after the first Discoveries of God to his Soul, at its introduction into his Body, is no Impeachment of the Divine Wisdom, as if God had not sufficiently reveal'd himself to him at first; because by the Consequence of the Thing it could not have been otherwise.

To what purpose should Christ have been reveal'd to Man in his upright perfect State? with what Efficacy could the Doctrine of Salvation, and the Notions of Redemption have been publish'd to him, who had not offended? *Adam* might well have reply'd to God himself, What occasion have I for all this?[92] I have always punctually observ'd the most righteous Law which thou hast given me, and resolve to observe it with the utmost exactness as long as I live.

The Reason of a MESSIAH is founded in the Delinquency of the Man, and could have no Place in the Nature of the Thing, till the Offence was committed; but then, we may even say there was a necessity of a farther Revelation than that which was at first made to him: Nay, if you will have it so, I might be allow'd to say, that God himself was oblig'd to make such a farther Revelation, or none at all; because to have reveal'd Christ as a promis'd Saviour, before the Man had sinn'd, and thereby stood in need of him, would have been inverting the Order of things,[93] and could not be done without the greatest Impropriety.

And what Weakness or Imperfection was there in all this? Not to reveal the Cure before the Wound was given; not to shew the Remedy before the Disease? On the contrary, it was highly consonant to, and agreeing with, all the ordinary Methods of Divine Wisdom; who having first established the due Order of things, and the Courses of Causes and Consequences, unalterable but by himself; is pleased, except in manifest Necessity, to make all the ordinary Courses, even of his own Providence, to observe and bend to those Courses of Cause and Consequence, and very rarely to anticipate Nature; and not at all, but upon extraordinary Occasions.

It remains to speak of the Necessity of a further Revelation, in this great Article of the Promise of a MESSIAH, and that Man could arrive to the Knowlege of it by no other way, which is the Subject of the next Chapter.

IIIIIIIIIIIIIIIIIIIIIIIIIIIIIIIIIIIIIIIIIIIIIIIIIIIIIIIIIIIIIIIIIIIIIIIIIIIIIIIIIIIIII

CHAP. V[a].

That the Promise of a MESSIAH *made to Man after his Fall, could be known by no other Method, but that of Revelation, and that all the Powers of his Reason could not lead him to the Discovery.*

MANY learned Men have spoken largely to this Point; namely, that tho' the Light of Man's Reason did lead him to just Notions of the Being of a God, and that it was a rational Consequence from thence, that this God was to be worshipped; yet that the most perfect degree of human Understanding, did not, and could not guide the Man to determine what kind of Homage and Adoration was to be paid to GOD, and with what kind of Worship he would be best pleased.[94]

This appears by the mean and weak Efforts of the most refin'd Understandings in the first Ages of Knowledge, when they came to act in matters of *Religious Worship*; in all which they run into the grossest Absurdities, practicing inhuman Cruelties, various and unheard of Barbarisms, unclean and filthy Customs, and even some unnatural, as sacrificing their own Children, to appease their Gods; all which, as they were inconsistent with Reason, so they were Unworthy of God, and only serve to testify that the meer Light of Reason is but dark and dim in the clearest Heads, till assisted by farther and farther Illuminations.

But I proceed; for this part, I say, has been largely spoken to by many learned Men, and by some eminent Divines on several Occasions, even against the Infidels of this Age: But I carry it on to one Circumstance more, which reaches the Case before me, in a manner very convincing.

If Reason, with its utmost Illuminations, could not discover to Mankind, how, and in what manner God would be worshipped, much less could it discover Christ to the Souls of Men: In this discovery there are so many amazing Wonders, that Reason is so far from being able to reveal them to herself, that she is hardly able to conceive of them, even when reveal'd to her from God.

I know some would make the Wonders of Redemption be a Reason against their Faith, and a Just Cause why they should not lay any stress upon it, a very wrong way of arguing, and fatal to the Souls of those who flie to it;

perplexing them with inextricable Doubts and Difficulties about accepting the offered Salvation, which it is their only eternal Felicity that they may accept.

I think, on the contrary, those Wonders which appear in the Gospel Revelation, should be so far from arguing against, that they assist to convince our Reason of the Necessity of its being an immediate Revelation; who, but the God whose Wisdom is unsearchable, and his Ways past finding out,[95] could have thought of, much less reveal'd, and offer'd to the fallen offending Creature in his Extremity, under the Sentence of THE DEATH, as it is emphatically exprest[96] in the Threatning, a Ransom by a MESSIAH, by an Offering equal to the Offence, and worthy the Acceptance of the Majesty offended? by what human Method could it have been assured to the Soul of the Man, and the Creature be brought to receive Comfort from it, in a condition of all that can be conceiv'd of the most miserable and disconsolate?

Could his Reason have suggested it to him, or any thing like it? Could he have form'd any Idea of it in his Mind? Take him in his most exalted Flights, opinionative and conceited,[97] as the worst of our present Deists and Free-Thinkers are: I am perswaded none of them, take them, I say, in the highest Notions that they can form for themselves, can say, they could have come up to it.

Let us endeavour to argue this Point upon the highest suggestions of Reason, and let them begin at the beginning of Things. They must grant us first, that Man, notwithstanding his reasoning Powers, did offend God, did fall; let them call it what they please; this was a Breach of the Law of Reason, and Reason might very well charge the Criminal: But that God would be pleas'd to forgive the Breach, and to accept him for the Rectitude of his future Conduct, what will Reason say to that? Nay, and that God must do this; that he could not require any more of his Creature than his Reason would direct, when as indeed he had not acted as his Reason did direct, but contrary to it: This his Reason could never dictate any more than how this forgiving Quality in God should be expected.

To say, therefore, if the Man sincerely pursues the Dictates of his Reason, God is bound to accept him, is saying Nothing; unless you will also venture to say, that he is bound to accept him, notwithstanding any Breach of his Obedience to that Reason; and to say that, is to say God is oblig'd to accept the Man, whether he does obey his Reason or no.

And here the Necessity of Revelation appears again, for tho' the Doctrine of a Satisfaction[98] by a Redeemer, be the most rational Scheme of Religion that could be thought of, and no rational Man ever objected against it on that Account; yet Reason could never dictate to Mankind, that his offended Maker would be propitiated after his Offence, any more than that it should be effected by a Sacrifice: Nor had the offering up thousands of Rams, and Ten thousands of Rivers of Oil,[99] or even the *fruit of the Body for the sins of the Soul*, had any thing rational in it; if God had not reveal'd from Heaven, that it was his Will to be thus approach'd by Man, as a Type of the great Offering mention'd above, of the Messiah; Which he had appointed for a Propitiatory Sacrifice, for the Sins of the World, and till HE should come, when all those Types were to cease, and be swallow'd up in the thing typified; all which was dictated to the Man, not by his Reason; for that was no way capable of so much Illumination, but it came to him directly from God; and if they will not call it Revelation, let them tell us what it is, and we will give them leave to call it what they please.

But let them call it what they will, they must also give us leave to call it Revelation, for such it is, and nothing else.

None of our Infidels, that I meet with, will say, they never offended their Maker, or that they have so sincerely adhered to the perfect Law of Reason, which they talk of, as to have made no Breach. Well, how then is that Breach to be made up? Is God indispensibly oblig'd to take their broken Obedience for perfect, to day sincere, to morrow insincere, to day acting rationally, to morrow brutally and immorally, is this a rational Scheme?

Or is it more probable that God being offended by the Immorality of yesterday, should reject and refuse your Obedience and Sincerity of to Day, till his Justice, angry as it was, and offended, should be satisfy'd for the Insult offered before? And how shall this be done? I may call upon Reason itself to speak, whether it ought to be done or no; and I may challenge all the Reason of Man to have found out a Propitiation equal to the Offence, and not unworthy of the Majesty of God to accept of, in the whole World.

In the Crisis of this Exigence,[100] God himself, for none else could conceive of it, brings to Light the glorious Medium of a Reconciliation by a propitiatory Sacrifice; namely, the Blood of Attonement, hence, justly, call'd the Blood *of the everlasting Covenant.* Heb. xiii. 20. and this he reveal'd to *Adam* in the moment of his Convictions, mercifully to prevent his Despair.

Let us go back to it again: Man had sinn'd, fallen from his first Rectitude, 'tis no matter how, or when, or in what manner; but he had sinn'd: Sinn'd against God and his own Reason: who should dictate to him that God was any thing but righteous, a just Judge, and as such, must execute the Sentence threatned upon him? Where had he the first Discoveries that God was merciful, and that he should be forgiven? I demand of these Men, whether

Adam's Reason could dictate that to him? when on the contrary God had expressly declar'd otherwise, in the threatning of Death, which was positive? it must suppose God to break that righteous Word, and not be infinitely just, if Death did not follow, for nothing could be more warmly exprest than the Commination is, IN THE DAY *thou offendest thou shalt surely die*, Gen. ii. 17. Nothing can be more awful and solemn than this Threatning, thou shalt SURELY or certainly DIE; and in the very Day; did *Adam's* Reason dictate to him that the God of Truth would break his Word? that would be to make his Reason be the Serpent that beguil'd them, for that was the very Bait the Serpent laid, and this is the Bait our Infidels at this Day lay for themselves, *viz.* God has threatned you indeed with Death, and Eternal Death; but do not believe that God can be so cruel, do not believe, (as they tell us King *Charles* the Second said,)[101] *That God who is a gracious and beneficent Being, will be so severe as to punish eternally for a few out of the way Pleasures*, not judging, as the Lord does, by the Corruption and Pollution of the Heart.

Now, if Reason thus gives the Lie to God's positive Threatnings, I must say Reason acts the Serpent upon us, and puts himself in the Devil's stead, to delude us to our Destruction.

God is a merciful and beneficent Being, his Mercy is his Glory, *'tis exalted above all his Name*;[102] but God's Mercy is exhibited in Christ only, and received and embraced by Faith in him, and by that only; Christ is the Channel from whence all those Streams flow, and thro' whom they are convey'd, his Blood is the Attonement, *and speaks better things than that of Abel*, Heb. xii. 24.

But supposing this, only by the way; how, *I say*, did Man first come to know that God would have Mercy on him, and forgive him, notwithstanding his capital Offence? Doubtless he knew he had offended God, when he said, I was afraid;[103] his Knowlege of Guilt appear'd many ways; but how did he know that God would have Mercy on him and forgive him, and that he should not die? It will be hard for them to assign any Method how he came to know this, but by Revelation from the very Mouth of God himself; where, in the Sentence on the Serpent, he promises Man's Redemption, *I will put enmity between thee and the Woman, and between thy Seed and her Seed, it shall bruise thy head, and thou shalt bruise his heel*, Gen. iii. 15a.

He knew so much of God, as to know he was just and righteous, as well as great and glorious; he had all the Reason in the World to believe, that what the just and holy Majesty of God had pronounced with so much solemn Asseveration, should be fulfilled, and that he should *surely die*.

Whence then had he any Comfort? Whence did he learn that God had pitied his Misery and would not destroy him, tho' he had deserv'd it, and

God had threatned it? nay, had, as we say, decreed it, tho', as it appear'd, not unalterably:[104] The Answer is plain, it must come to him from the Mouth of God, and that is Revelation, or nothing can be so.

This we might turn upon the Adversary, and give our Work the Title of *Revelation as old as the Creation*; for as the reasoning Powers, given to Man with his Soul, were a Revelation, or Inspiration, and that the Promise of Christ upon the Fall, was a subsequent Revelation; we may well say, that Christianity, or the Knowlege of, and Faith in Christ, which is the only real and true Christianity, are as old as the Fall of Man, that is to say, as old as the Tryal and Conviction of the Three Criminals; *to wit*, the Man, the Woman, and the Devil.

Here Christ was reveal'd to *Adam*, as a Sacrifice, as if really and already offered up, and from the beginning accepted; and hence Christ is truly call'd, *the Lamb slain from the foundation of the World*, Rev. xiii. 8. This Mr. *Milton* represents in a most sublime Light,[105] by the Son moving his Father in a most tender and compassionate manner, to have pity upon his weak offending Creature Man; and to spare him and lay the Weight of the Curse denounced, in case of a Fall, all upon himself; and this is happily exprest by the Apostle St. *Paul*, that he *was made a curse for us*, Gal. iii. 13. And the same Text tells us how, namely, that he took the Curse denounced upon Man, to himself: He redeemed us from the Curse of the Law, *being*, or BY *being, made a Curse for us*.

I might desire my Readers to pause, or stop here awhile, and wait to hear, what in all this it was possible the utmost Wit of Man could find to cavil at, and to raise Objections upon; Nothing to me can appear more irresistible than the Truth of this Assertion; namely, that Christ was revealed from Heaven to our first Parents, as the Propitiation for their Guilt; that God had accepted him as the Mediator, the one and only Mediator between God and Man, the man *Christ Jesus*.[106]

This Revelation was after the Fall, not before it, therefore all the Mind and Will of God concerning Man, was not laid down fully to him before his Fall; for his Disobedience being a Fact subsequent to his Creation, it could not be: There was no Christ, no Redeemer or Redemption till there was a lapse or falling first, no Pardon is past before the Offence is committed.

It is not consistent with Reason that Christ should be revealed to *Adam* before he had transgress'd. No, no, *Adam*, in the utmost confusion of Shame and Despair, fled from the sight of his offended Creator, expecting nothing but immediate Death, according to the Terms of the Law given him; he might well say he was naked, for he was stript of his Innocence, that spotless

Robe in which his Maker had at first cloathed him; and when GOD called him, and he was forc'd to come forth and hold up his Hand, as we might call it,[107] what did he do? He came trembling, pleaded guilty, confest the Indictment; but not a word of crying for Mercy, no kneeling down, beseeching God to forgive him; no, but talk'd like a Fool,[108] laid the fault upon his Wife, the Woman that thou gavest to be with me *she gave it me*;[109] and she does the same, and lays it upon the Devil, *the Serpent beguiled me*.[110]

I chuse to relate this in the Terms of the sacred Text; because, it will for ever be to me the genuine History of the Fact; whether in Allegory or not, is not material to the Case;[111] let the Infidels we talk of, reject the manner, if they please, they can never reject the substance of the History; namely, that the first Man offended God, and that by one Man, sin entered into the World, and Death by sin, and that Christ was reveal'd immediately as the Mediator between God and Man, to redeem him from the Curse,[112] or the Man had immediately, in virtue of the Curse pronounc'd, been destroy'd.

As they acknowlege the Offence, they must acknowlege the Redemption, or they will be at a loss to answer this Question, Why the Sentence was not executed? If they fly to this, which is their usual shift, *viz.* That it was the meer Mercy and Benignity of God; we join with them in that: But then, where is the Immutability of his Holiness and Justice, who had spoken, and could not go back, *that he should surely die*? Certainly die! and so he did, by the Son of God interposing and taking the stroke upon himself: So that he, by the Grace, that is, *the mercy* of God, might taste Death for every Man, *Heb.* ii. 9.

I suppose, by this time, the Author of *Christianity as old as the Creation*, will explain himself thus; That he means Christianity is no other Religion than the same that has been ever since the Creation; but this will not stand him in any stead, for even that way it is an Error in itself: For Christianity is the Doctrine of Salvation by a Redeemer, and at the Creation the Religion of *Adam* was the Doctrine of Righteousness upon a compleat Obedience; THIS supposes a Rectitude of the Soul, shining in perfect and spotless Innocence: That supposes the Soul polluted with Crime, under the Terror of an irretrevable Guilt, and the Weight of a dreadful Sentence; but, receiv'd to Mercy thro' the Intercession of a blessed Mediator, whose sacrifice of himself is accepted of God the offended, and the Offender is ransom'd and justify'd for his sake. This is the glorious Scheme of redeeming Grace, and the Profession of Faith, in this reveal'd Religion, is Christianity, and nothing else; so that to say, Christianity is nothing but the Religion of Reason, is a falshood, and has no Truth in it; no, nor any pretence of Truth, for it is quite another thing; and to say, it is as antient as the Creation, is likewise a falshood; because, as has been prov'd, there was a time when it was not, when the Doctrine of a Christ, or a Redeemer was *not*; that is to say, was not heard of, was not wanted, was not in the Nature of the Thing.

This being the Case, the enquiry how the Christian Doctrine came into the World, which is the necessary Consequence of the thing, introduces the present Proposition; namely, that it was by Revelation from God, that it could be no other way; that the Reason of Man could not have reach'd it, or by any of its most perfect exalted Operations have led Mankind to such a Discovery.

I see no way our Infidels have to come off of this; but to turn Pagan, and with *Epicurus*, not only to deny that the first Man offended, but to deny that there was any first Man at all; that all things ever were what they are, and ever will be just the same; which is the Doctrine of the Eternity of the World;[113] a Notion too gross to deserve a reply, and too ridiculous to bring into a Discourse so solemn and serious[114] as this.

That there was a first beginning of all terrestrial Being, is granted by Christians, and I am not now engaged with the Platonick or Epicurean Philosophy, or Philosophers; but with such as at least call themselves Christians, and to those I address myself thus:

If there was no Offence committed by *Adam*, or call him by what Name you will, pray then, who was the first Sinner, and when did Sin enter the World? For we find it is in the very Man as a Creature, twisted with his very Soul, his very Reason, which is pretended to be his Infallible Guide, is corrupted and debauch'd; now whence is it, and how comes it to be so, and what time did it begin? For if it was not always so, then it had a beginning; this would be a noble Discovery, and would lead us to the Knowlege of many Things of the greatest Importance for us to know.

Nor would it be sufficient to know when Crime came first into the World. But how came it into the Man? How had this Legion Power to enter into the Herd?[115] We find it is not only in some, but in all; it is not this or that Man, or a few Men that are wicked, but, in short, Mankind are tainted; the whole Race is touch'd with the Infirmity; Death passed upon all Men; for that all have sinned.[116] How comes it to pass? it does not run in the Blood, for that is Nature; but in the Life and Spirit, in the very Soul? Whence is this general Depravity, and where did it begin?

If there was such a Golden Age, when this was not the Case, when Men were not by innate Principles addicted to Crime; when Corruption had taken no hold of Mankind; when was it, and how long did it last, and which way came the glorious State of Things to be overthrown and reduc'd, as we now see it is, to the grossest Part of the Iron Age,[117] corrupted and deprav'd, fill'd with Violence, Fraud, Pride, Envy, distemper of the Soul, and Death?

I do not now ask them when Men did strictly obey, and sincerely adhere to the Dictates of their own Reason, tho' even that would perplex them to give an Answer to. But to bring it home to them at once, I ask, When had Reason such Powers? when did it enjoy the full and free exercise of its own Powers, if it had such, so as to guide Mankind perfectly to please his Creator, or to do all that God could expect of him? And lastly, when did our Reason lose that Power? Certainly it is not now possess of any such Power, but Man in the highest Exercise of his Reason, commits daily Offences against God, and such as Reason it self will acknowlege to be such.

In a word, these Men must acknowlege a first Man, or they will be unable to find out an Original for Crime; and especially for the Universality of Crime; and above all, for its being, as above, gotten into the very Soul of the Creature, mixt with his Understanding, and possest of all his reasoning Powers, and Faculties. How comes the original Propensity to offend,[118] and whence is it prevalent, even against the opposition, which in some Cases Reason makes against it? I leave them to reply to these things at leisure.

But suppose, tho' not granting, that according to these Men, there was no Christ, horrid suggestion! yet such as they are not asham'd of, no Revelation from Heaven; tho' indeed, they must give up Reason it self with that Supposition; for, as above, 'tis evident, she has no Knowlege, how to serve or worship God, but by Revelation; But suppose it, I say, for Argument sake, how should we, then, suggest any such thing as Mercy and Forgiveness in God, who we allow to be a righteous, holy and just Being?

How also must we suggest, that He, who is essential Truth itself, should falsify his Word, and not make good his threatned Anger? How shall promis'd Mercy be expected, when promis'd Vengeance is not executed? What kind of a God must we make of him:

Who is so merciful, he can't be just?[119]

But to return: From what Principle can we suggest that God will pardon our Offences without Repentance, without Reformation, without a Satisfaction, without a Saviour or Sacrifice? And whence must the Notion of such Benignity in the Nature of God arise.

It is evident his Vengeance against Offenders is often declared with Terror, *the wrath of God is reveal'd from Heaven against all unrighteousness,*[120] Rom. i. 18. But where shall we look for his Mercy? if the Revelation of Christ is not, if a Saviour is not, Reveal'd Mercy cannot; for Salvation without a Saviour is utterly inconsistent with the righteous and just Nature of God; there was no Attonement without a Sacrifice, no Sacrifice without a Priest, no Priest without an Altar, no Altar without a Mercy Seat;[121] the Climate is the same, and holds even from the beginning.

The first Man offended God: Death enter'd by Sin, and Death came upon all, in that all have sinned: The Contagion has reached the whole Race; with this dreadful blast of Crime, the healing Breath of a promis'd Salvation came on, and Man was redeemed by an accepted Sacrifice. 'Tis strange the rational Part of this Œconomy of Mercy should not convince Men, and that their Reason should not bring them, by the force of its own Light, to acknowlege the Lustre of the Doctrine of Reconciliation: But we harden our Hearts, and shut our Eyes against our own Reason, while at the same time we would erect that very Reason as our only Guide: Preposterous Creatures! to set up that Reason for an Idol, which refuses the Idolatry, and abhors the Crime of it!

In a word, all Religion is Revelation, *Adam*, in his Innocent State, had the Law and Will of his Maker reveal'd to him, internally to his Reason, and externally to his Senses, by Voice; that is, by the Appearance of God, or an Angel of God, speaking audibly, and giving him a Law.

After his Fall he had a new Religion dictated to him, namely, that of Faith and Repentance, an offer of Mercy, and a promis'd Seed being made to him in the same manner, namely, by Voice; and at the same time reveal'd to his Soul by the Grace and Spirit of God.

If all this was not Revelation, and that a farther and farther Revelation, which went on till Life and Immortality came to Light; that is to say, was reveal'd by the Gospel; I say, if it was not all Revelation, it was not at all in Fact; and so Christ and Salvation by him, which is the only true Christianity, is nothing but a Delusion; and, indeed, they do as good as acknowlege it is so; wretched People as they are! God of his infinite Mercy open their Eyes, that the Light of the glorious Gospel of *Jesus Christ* may shine into their Hearts, 2 *Cor.* iv. 4.

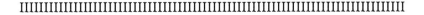

CHAP. VIª.

That if the Revelation of all Religion is from God, it is highly just and Conso-nant to our Reason that it should be believ'd, and that we should be obedient to the heavenly Vision.

HAVING, I think, establish'd this Truth, that all true Religion has its rise in Revelation, and at least that the Christian religion is thus founded: We should enquire in the next place, what we mean by this awful word Revela-tion, what it is, and from whence the things that are thus reveal'd do proceed.

Now to do this, in a summary way, yet so as may stand its ground against the gainsayers of the Age, I shall explain the word Revelation, not in its literal or grammatical Acceptation, but as it is ordinarily understood by even our Opponents in this Dispute; namely, the written Word, which we call, and that rightly too, *the Word of God*, or the Scriptures; as being the Word by which GOD has reveal'd his Mind and Will to Men, and wherein he has laid them down a rule of Life and Doctrine, which if they follow, they may expect all the Blessings promis'd therein.

The Essence and Substance of this written Word is summ'd up in this, (*viz.*) That it is the *everlasting Gospel*[122] reveal'd from Heaven, preach'd to Mankind by the Son of God himself, and confirm'd to us by them that heard him, *God also bearing them witness by signs and wonders, and divers miracles and Gift of the Holy Ghost, according to his Will*, Heb. ii. 4.

If these Men demand of us, how we know the Scripture is the Word and Will of God, and how we know the Revelation is from him? I answer in the like summary way; but let them confute it if they can; *because it has discovered* (that is, Revealed) *those things to Man* which *none but God could know*;[123] of this the number of Instances are too great to need any mention; but the whole Tenour of the Old Testament Prophecies and Promises are full of them; and the whole body of the New Testament History, is a Testimonial of their being punctually fulfill'd.[124]

The Demonstrations of this Truth, and the Discoveries of God, of which every part of the Scripture is full, would take up not a Chapter, but a Volume to repeat; I leave it upon the Affirmative above-mention'd, which I undertake to support against all the Cavils of the Age, be they as great as they will.

Supposing it then capable of such support, which it must be, till what I have here alledged is confuted; I infer in the words of the blessed Apostle, 1 Tim. i. 15. *It is a faithful saying, and worthy of all acceptation.*[125]

In a word, if the Christian Religion is a Revelation, and is from God, let us see the Man that can be so audacious, as to say, *it ought not to be receiv'd*, to be embrac'd with the highest Veneration, and believ'd with the utmost Sincerity and Resignation? Can they own it to be the word of God, and not believe it! 'tis a preposterous Boldness! it arms Heaven and Earth against them, and sets Conscience and Reason in a perfect Flame.

It is far from a Confutation of this Fundamental, to say, there are some Difficulties in the reading, seeming Contradictions, wrong Translations, Errors in the Copies, and the like; let them come to the Point, let them recognize that which is plain, congruous, undeniable, and against which no such Objection lies, and they will find enough of that to command their Awe, and to establish the Reverence of God and Religion in their Minds;[126] they will find the very Image of God stampt upon every part of it, all its Commands come with a visible Signature of the Divine Authority;[127] they establish Virtue, Piety, Meekness, Humility, and Self-denial; they exalt every generous and beneficent Principle; they attract Reverence to the Being which has created us, and direct in what manner to serve and honour him, so as to be accepted by him, and to be made for ever happy with him.

They discourage every Vice, every thing that is in the least disagreeable to the Laws of Reason, to the Good of human Society, or repugnant to the strictest Honour and Truth; they condemn every thing that is evil, unworthy of the Man as a rational Creature, or unworthy of God, the Giver of his Being, and end of his Life.

If it were the word of a Man, the Failings and Imperfections of human Nature, would some where or other appear; whereas here is nothing but a most righteous Law, a most perfect Rule, and all leading to the most happy End: if it were the word of a Man, it would bewray its Author by its Imperfections,[128] and might, for that Reason alone[a], be doubted; but as it is from God, its whole Tenour is like its Author, one body of uniform Truth, every where directing to the best End, by the most direct and infallible means, a Testimony of its proceeding from the Mouth of him, who is himself the essential Light of Truth, the GOD of TRUTH,[129] yea TRUTH it self.

Whatever is spoken with such an Authority, ought to be believ'd, as whatever is commanded by him that is himself essential Truth, ought to be submitted to and obey'd.

This being laid down as a Proposition, and I believe it is receiv'd as such, it follows then, at least, that the Evidence of Scripture be receiv'd; that is, that the Testimony of Scripture be admitted in Evidence on the Trial of the Cases before us, (*viz.*) That the Scripture History, which is so evidently confirm'd by the Voice of God, and so frequently quoted and referr'd to, even by Christ himself, should be believ'd as Authentic; its Authority allow'd, the Facts it relates and attests admitted to be True, and receiv'd as such.

It farther infers, that all the Scripture Prophecies, especially such as we find have had their Accomplishment in the Gospel Times, and are apparently fulfill'd, should be acknowleged, as so many glorious Testimonials, or Certificates, to the Verity of the ancient Revelation, and the Preachings of inspir'd Men in all Ages.

What a wonderful Concurrence of Circumstance[130] do we meet with in Scripture, in the things predicted, and the things fulfill'd; it would fill a Volume to remark how the promis'd Deliverances arriv'd to a Day, at the distance of many hundred Years, and the threatned Judgments, with the same exactness, the self-same Day, says the Text:[131] Threatned Deluge, long before it came; and when it was near, 'tis said, yet seven Days, *and I will cause it to rain,* &c. Gen. vii. 4.[132] The low Condition, and Captivity of the *Israelites*, expressly stated to a Day, and their Deliverance, as above, fixt and perform'd to that very appointed Day. The casting down *Jeroboam*'s Altar, and polluting it, by burning the Bones of Men upon it; how circumstantially was it predicted, even to the Name of the King that should perform it (*Josiah* by Name) and how exactly was it fulfill'd;[133] the destruction of *Jerusalem*, and the captivity in *Babylon*, the time of it, the continuance of it, (*viz.*) 70 Years, the return from it, the glory of the second Temple, the coming of the MESSIAH into that Temple, and at last the final Destruction of it, and the scattering the whole Nation; how were they exactly foretold, and all that was foretold, most exactly fulfill'd?[134]

If this can be done by the hand of Man, or by any human Art, I would gladly hear some Examples of the kind, and some intimation of any Person who ever pretended to it: Even the Devil, whose Power of Prediction, some have suggested to be great, tho' Reason dictates, that there is nothing of that kind in his Power,[135] could not reach to these wonderful things, nor to any thing like them.

I omit abundance of other Prophecies, and prophetic Visions, of which the several Books of *Daniel, Ezekiel*, and others, are full, and in which the several Revolutions of Empires and Monarchies in the World are so exactly foretold, many of which are already fulfill'd, and others, yet behind, are in a fair prospect of being fulfill'd, concluding it all with this particular Observation, (*viz.*) That where an appointed time, for the fulfilling of any one Prediction in Scripture is precisely set down, they cannot give one Example where that time has elaps'd, without a fulfilling of the thing predicted.

Are not these marks of a Divine Impression?[136] Are not these eminent Signatures of the high Original of the Scriptures, and sufficient to satisfy any reasonable Inquirer? and if they are such, they must necessarily command our belief of its Contents.

The sum of this whole Discourse may then be contained in these few Generals.

1. The first Impressions of religious Knowlege on the Minds of Men, were by the secret Operation of GOD revealing himself to the Soul.
2. *Christianity*, or the Religion of JESUS, which tho' not as antient as the Creation, is yet as old as the Sentence past upon the Fall of Man, is a farther Revelation of God to Man, deliver'd to him vocally in Paradise, before his being expell'd from thence.
3. *This farther Revelation*; namely, the Revelation of a Redemption by a promis'd Saviour, which is *Christianity*, being audibly deliver'd to the first Man, from God himself, is therefore not unworthy of God, or inconsistent with the Holiness, Goodness, and unchangeable Perfections of his Being; if it had,[137] he would not have made such a farther Revelation, and if one subsequent Revelation, was not unworthy of God, inconsistent or incredible, then other, and farther Revelations of his Mind and Will to Man, may be equally worthy, consistent, and to be believ'd, as coming from himself.
4. *The Scripture* is a farther and continued Revelation of the Mind and Will of God; is a perfect rule of Life to Man, and for his Guidance in serving and worshipping God, in order to his own eternal Felicity, and may be therefore worthy of God, and consistent with all his unchangeable Perfections.

These things being laid down as Fundamentals, it follows, that full Credit is to be given to this subsequent Revelation, and the whole Scripture is to be receiv'd with a due Veneration, and an intire Credence;[138] it is to be believ'd as a written Word inspir'd from God, and that as such, is really the Word of God, and contains so much of his Mind and Will concerning us, as is sufficient for our Eternal Salvation. In a word, according to what is quoted above from the blessed Apostle St. *Paul*, if *it is a faithful saying*, it is *worthy of all acceptation*, 1 Tim. i. 15ᵃ.

The Opposers of these Truths, cannot avoid the force of this reasoning, (*viz.*) That if the Scripture is the word of God, it ought to be believ'd; and therefore they turn back upon the Scripture itself, and raise Cavils at the Text, that they may avoid the Consequence.

On the other hand, to come a little closer to these Men, in this particular part, (*viz.*) their disputing the Veracity of the Scripture, it must be said of them, that they show a dreadful Indifference in things of the utmost weight and consequence, even to themselves.

For suppose, *as we may well do*, that the Scripture should be the word of GOD, and that it is a real Revelation of his *Mind* and *Will*; what Condition will these Men find themselves in then? and thus far is a certain Truth, and I think they will not dispute it, (*viz.*) that they are not sure of the Negative; nay, I will venture to go farther, the Affirmative is reasonable, the Negative only presumptive;[139] that it is so, is probable; that it is not so is doubtful; and on which side lies the hazard? either there is no danger in the Negative, or these Men are unaccountably negligent of themselves, and strangely quiet and tranquil in the greatest imaginable Risque.[140]

I am not ignorant of the innumerable Cavils and Scruples they raise daily to support their Infidelity, and to buoy themselves in their opposition to the Divine Authority of the sacred Text: I think they need no reply in this place, let them first get over what I have insisted on here; namely, of itsᵃ revealing or discovering such things, which none but God could know, and their Cavils may be encountred afterwards; let them tell us, what human Prescience could foretel things so remote in Time, so particular in Circumstance, as the Scripture does, and which have so critically been fulfill'd; let them give the least rational Account of any other Power, from Earth or Hell, that could do this, and we may give up some Points to them.

The Books of the Sybils, the Oracles of the Heathen, the Conjurations of the Magicians:[141] What were they all? And how often did they fail in their Predictions? But here they cannot assign one Mistake, one false Prediction, not one jot or tittle[142] of this word has fail'd; not one word has fallen to the ground,[143] and Heaven and Earth shall pass away, e'er one word of it shall fail; to what End do Men strain their Wits to find flaws in the Translation, and to form Objections, and seeming Contradictions in the several Versions, while they cannot undermine or destroy the Foundation?

The Reasonableness of a farther Revelation; nay, the Necessity of it, has a Sanction from the plain Fact; namely, that the first progressive Revelation was pronounc'd from the Mouth of God; if they deny this, they must deny the first Promise of a *Messiah*; nay, the *Messiah* himself; and yet this Author talks of a Religion call'd Christianity, as if there could be any Christianity without a Christ; if then, he will own any such thing as a Christianity, he must own, as above, that it was a Revelation from the Mouth of God, subsequent to the first Revelation of God, in, and unto the rational Soul: If not, let him show us what he means by Christianity, and why he gives it that Name, a Name which really does not belong to it.

That there may be Abuses and Corruptions of reveal'd Religion, I shall not dispute, nor are those Abuses and Corruptions any way our concern in this present Debate; let the Reverence due to the Revelation itself, be first establish'd, and the main point granted, that it is from God, all the mistakes about it, or about our own Conduct, on that Account, may be debated afterward. While the Reason of Man is fallible, and his Judgment corrupt, Mistakes will follow, and Man will err; but this is no Impeachment of the Wisdom of God,[144] in giving a farther Revelation, but rather, on the contrary, shews the necessity of it.

Thus far, I think, all the tedious and formal Schemes, of what we would have called rational Religion, are answer'd at once, and the Antiquity of Christianity is settled, as also, that Christianity itself, is a Revelation, and that a farther and subsequent Revelation being since the Fall of Man, and since the Degeneracy of his reasoning Powers, which appear every day deficient and unable to preserve him from offending, and much more unable to make reparation for the Offence committed.

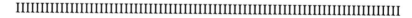

CHAP. VII[a].

An Enquiry into the End and Design of all the Cavils which are made at, and the Warmth that is exerted against reveal'd Religion, and whether they tend to make Men more Religious, or less.

ONE of the best Testimonies, to the Goodness of any Profession, is, that it has a direct Tendency to make Men better: I shall always suspect the Truth of that Opinion, or of that Religion, which makes Men worse, and not better; a holy Life is the rational Consequence of a holy Religion, and of a sincere Profession of it.

If it could be made appear, that these Cavils about Religion, and these Doubts about the Truth of Religion , had a suitable effect on the Lives of Men, and that those who made these Objections, were made better by the Enquiry, if it tended to make them more serious, and more religious, we might be a little prejudic'd in their Favour; but if, on the contrary, these suggestions have a tendency to make Men less religious, less pious, and less earnest after the felicity of a future State, it argues strongly against them, that they are not in a right pursuit of the thing itself; that they act upon a wrong Foundation, in which they meet with no Blessing.

How mean, how wretched a View is it, that those People act from, in an Affair of this Consequence, whose end is popularity and applause? who dare blaspheme God, and make a mock of things sacred, to be talk'd up among Men, and to pass for something extraordinary? Sure such Men cast off all Religion at once.

We are told, the *Religion of Nature*, that is to say, of *Reason*, consists in observing those things, which our Reason, by considering the Nature of God and Man, and the relation we stand in to him, and to one another, demonstrates to be our Duty.[145]

This is a strange Jargon of Words, without much real signification; for how should our Reason consider the Nature of God, and the relation we stand in to him, without the help of some Revelation, some secret Light shining into it from God, to discover himself to the Man? But, let it stand as it is, and let us go on with it thus; the *Religion of Reason* consists in observing, &c. but what if the culpable Man, with all the Light of his Reason, does not, or has not observ'd these things, which Reason demonstrates to be his Duty, what do all the fine things these Men say of God, tend to as that he is a Being absolutely perfect, and infinitely happy in himself; that he did not create Man for his own sake, or command them any thing for his own interest or advantage, or to no end or purpose, nor for any thing but for their own good, and the like; what, I say, do they all amount to but this, that God, who is infinitely happy in himself, is not better'd by our Obedience, nor does he stand in need of our Services, all which, we most readily allow.

But what is all this to our Rebellion and Disobedience?[146] Does this prove that God cannot resent, that 'tis below him to be angry; that he is so good that he can't be just, that he is not a jealous God,[147] visiting his Creatures,[148] and afflicting them for their Offences? I see not one word of Divine Justice, but God is so good a Being, that he is above all anger or resentment, can do himself no Justice upon the most impious Offender, and yet how many dreadful Testimonies has God given in the World of his Anger and Vengeance against crying Offences?

How does he often testify his abhorrence of the Criminal, as well as of the Crime, and snatch Men immediately from Life, in the very act of offending him? as if to tell us, that he takes them into his own hand, to punish them farther as they deserve.

I have often observ'd how glorious a Testimony the God of Heaven and Earth gives, to those humble Souls that fear and serve him; that he is able to hear their Prayers, and what an encouragement it is to every Christian that prays to him; that we often find him hearing the horrid Blasphemies of his hardned Enemies, and as it were, obeying the Voice of their loud Imprecations,[149] when they call upon him to destroy them, and letting that Vengeance loose, which they impiously provoke to fall upon them.

Every Age is full of Examples sufficient to make a Deist tremble, if not too much hardened, when Divine Justice has struck dead the perjur'd Wretches that have call'd God to witness to a Lye.[150] How eminent is the ordinary Method of his Justice in pursuing the Murtherer, often bringing him even to detect himself, and be the Instrument of his own just Punishment?[151]

It is impossible these Men should resist the open Discoveries of Divine Vengeance upon desperate Criminals, and how it is so pointed, and so tim'd, that we have frequent Examples, where the Crime has been seen in the very Punishment;[152] and yet all this even by our own Reason, perfectly reconcilable to the Goodness and Benignity of God, and in the highest degree magnifies his Mercy, in that he does not oftner, or always, vindicate his Holiness in the same manner.

How do these Men lay a snare for their own Souls,[153] as well as for the Souls of their weaker Brethren, by pretending to exalt the Mercy and Goodness of God, in bar of his Holiness, and plead his infinite Goodness in arrest of Judgment,[154] for the most flagrant Offences? Is this a rational Religion! Can Reason suggest, that because God is good, that therefore we may act as we please, and that he will not take Vengeance upon us, if we sin against him, because he is good? As if God could not reconcile his Goodness with his detestation of Crime, and make all his Attributes conform together, without the least Contradiction; to what height of Impiety must such Notions lead the World? And how do they evidently tend to take away all that, which we justly call the Fear of God, out of the Minds of Men?

Their new Doctrines, of following the Dictates of Reason, as the Guide of the Soul, are so far from making the World better, that it is too evident they make it worse; for it gives them a loose in all manner of Levities, and even of the worst of Vices,[155] thro' the Error of their debauch'd Reasonings; not allowing that their Reason may be, and is often, darkned, if not entirely blinded, by the rage of Appetite,[156] and that they are hurried down the stream of their Affections[157] and Passions, in spite of whatever opposition their reasoning Powers are able to make.

Could they, indeed, advance, that their Reason was never misguided, never corrupted; cou'd they suggest that their WILLS always submitted to their UNDERSTANDINGS, that is to say, to their Reason, and the last was so steady a Rule of Life, that they either could not, or did not err; something might be said in their favour; but then such an Opinion must be supported by the proofs of Fact, and they must be able to appeal to their constant behaviour and conduct in Life; in which if all these concurred, they certainly would be the most blameless and upright Generation that the World ever saw.

But does this appear, is there any such thing to be seen among them? They tell us, they may answer all the great ends of Life, and all that God expects from them, if they do but pursue the Measures which their own Reason dictates; but where is the Man that does thus pursue the dictates of his Reason? Where the exactness of Conduct which might be expected from them, and what do they say about their slips and mistakes? They have not one word in all their rational System of what they are to do, or what they are to expect God will do, upon the many gross, foul, Affronts offer'd both to him their Maker, and to their own Reason, which was to be their Guide.

Repentance is not so much as nam'd among them; and as for a Sacrifice or Propitiation, 'tis all a Mockery, and mock'd at in all the rational Schemes they lay down; and yet they go on to Trespass, go on to Affront the Majesty of God, and insult his Goodness, and that with all the Tranquility imaginable; these things are so inconsistent with the very Notion of Religion in general, as well as with the Pretences they make to a rectitude of Soul, that I cannot see how they can reconcile them.

Certainly, that Religion which has a real Tendency to make the World worse, and not better, cannot claim to be the best, and truest Religion: A holy exact humble Life is the Consequence of a true Religion, and the Christian Religion boasts of its singularity, in recommending such Principles to Mankind, more than any other Religion. *He that has this hope in him, purifies himself, even as God is pure,* 1 John iii. 3. Let it come to the Test, do the Deists or the Christians purify themselves most, after the sacred Pattern; who live the most exact Lives, who walk by the best Rule?

We are told, that to entertain Notions of God, as an offended angry Judge, is to take away our love of God, and by our fear to bring ourselves to hate him; but this is an extreme which I see no necessity of our running into at all, and it is much more rational to suggest, that to suppose the goodness of God so to swallow up his Attribute of Justice, that the most obstinate Rebellion cannot move him to resent, is not only arguing against Reason, but against the experience of all Ages, wherein Testimonies of Divine Vengeance has been given, too apparent to be deny'd, and yet without Impeachment of the infinite Goodness, so essential to the Being of a God; and I think both these Attributes so consistent with the Being and Perfection of God, that the harmony of them is the most beautiful Contemplation in the World.

To deny the Justice of God, in vindication of his Mercy, is to make them absolutely repugnant to one another, which it is evident from numberless Examples, are reconcil'd in the whole Tenour of the Government of Providence in the World; and this may, indeed, serve for a full Answer to a whole Volume, swell'd with flourishes upon the Goodness and Beneficence of God, and telling us, that all thoughts of his Anger and Resentment, be the Cause ever so great, are unworthy of God.

The Question seems to be fully answer'd, by demonstration of Fact, against which it is to no purpose to argue:[158] Has the Wrath of God been reveal'd from Heaven, or has it not? And has it been evidently so reveal'd, against the unrighteousness of Men, or has it not? If it has, God has certainly reconcil'd his Vengeance and his Mercy, and by causing them to move in their several and respective Spheres, has made them consistent with one another, whether we can reconcile our thoughts of them or no.

If Men will dare to offend on the Presumption, that God is so good that he cannot resent, I think that Presumption detracts more from God, than any other false Notion of God can do; particularly as it tends to raze out the fear of God from the Minds of Men,[159] and leave every Man to walk in his own Ways,[160] being a Rule to himself; For if the Goodness and Benefi-cence of God is such, so incomprehensibly great, that he will take no notice of our Offences; nay, not of the vilest Contempt which we can offer to his most righteous Laws; what Inference is more rational than this, that then every Man may live as he pleases? As when there was no King in *Israel*, every Man did what was right in his own Eyes,[161] so when we can perswade our selves, that there are no Thunders in Heaven, no Vengeance to be fear'd from thence, we shall all do the like.

Nor is the Case without Testimony in the daily Practice of the Age; who are more profligate and more prophane, who lead more vicious Lives, and practice all manner of odious Crimes, than the Patrons of these Deistic Notions? How do they argue a full liberty in Crime, from the Benignity of Heaven, and the original Goodness of God, who can never be supposed to be angry with his Creatures, for gratifying those Affections and Passions, which he has plac'd in them: Nay, we find them arguing that he approves of all their wild Extravagances; because he does not immediately let fly his Anger, so the Mercy of God is abused and improv'd, to the support of Vice; and thus we find it was of old, *Ps.* l. 21. *These things hast thou done, and I kept silence: thou thoughtest, that I was altogether such a one as thy self: but I will reprove thee, and set them in order before thine Eyes.* I think I cannot close this Work better than by adding what the Holy Ghost says by the Royal Psalmist, in the very next verse to that quoted above, *viz.* Psalm l. 22. *Consider this, ye that forget* GOD, *least I tear you in pieces, and there be none to deliver.*

APPENDIX;

Affectionately address'd to the Youth of this Age, to prevent, if possible, their being early debauch'd with Atheistic and Deistic Principles.

HE must have no Compassion for the Souls of Men, and no Concern for the eternal Welfare of his Fellow-Creatures, who can be a silent and unmoved Spectator of the unhappy State of Religion at this time among us.

Innumerable Schisms and Divisions, Sects and Opinions, have for many Years torn and rent the Church of Christ, in a manner justly to be lamented; and I cannot without Grief reflect on what I have both heard and read, from the Mouths and Pens of some of the most learned, pious, and zealous Ministers of this Protestant Church, of their just Fears, that the Divisions and Breaches in religion, the Immorality of its Professors, and the Decay of the ancient Zeal for God, which was once the Glory of the Reformation, would at last open a door for such Errors, and give such a loose to the Lusts of Men, as, without the infinite Mercy of God interposing to prevent it, would overthrow the Establishment of Religion among us, and in the end ruin the Reformation it self.

We seem to be arriv'd at the unhappy time; we see Divisions in Opinion, Separations in religious Worship, Errors in Doctrine, and Breaches in Christian Charity, have broken in upon the Practice of Christians of almost all Denominations; and we have so mangled Religion it self, smother'd it with Errors, and torn it with our Passions and Prejudices, that it is as it were lost among us, at least it seems to be withdrawn from our Sight.

The Fear of God, which is the beginning of all religious Wisdom,[162] is rejected, the Terror of *his Anger* is lost, and the Edge of his Sword taken off, by our advancing new Notions of his Being and Attributes; erecting his Goodness, not only above all his Name,[163] but upon the Ruin of it; divesting him not only of all Resentment, but even of his Justice and Holiness; and supposing that because he does not, therefore he cannot strike; that he may be insulted, rebelled against, nay even deny'd and contemn'd, and yet that he is so infinitely good, he cannot be provok'd, and that he can only pity the Criminal not punish him.

I address this to the young People, the rising Generation of this Day; because as these horrid Notions of a God are craftily calculated by the harden'd, because unpunish'd, Offenders of the declining Age, for the pleasing and gratifying the youthful Inclinations, and most early Appetite of the growing Age, they have a greater occasion of timely Cautions, and the most earnest Remonstrances against being drawn in, to the Ruin of their Souls.

Knowing therefore the terror of the Lord, we perswade men. They are the Words of the blessed Apostle St. *Paul*, 2 *Cor.* v. 11. whose Affection for the Souls of Men was so very remarkable, and his Success in perswading them so great, that he converted thousands from the grossest heathen Idolatries and Errors of Paganism, to the Faith of a crucified Jesus, and established the most flourishing Churches that ever were in the World.

We take his Rule to perswade and exhort, and, if you please, from his own Mouth to direct, and the Direction is short; *search the Scriptures, and see* there, with the noble *Berozar, whether these things are so.*[164]

The Broachers of the Deistic Notions, which delude so many young Gentlemen, and encourage them at this time in their total Neglect of all Religion, oppose this with all their skill; they knew very well, that they could build up nothing if they could not pull down the Scripture; but *the Foundation of God standeth sure.*[165] We trust this is a Building which is of God, and shall for ever stand:[166] Heaven and Earth shall pass away, but not one Tittle of *his Word* shall fall to the Ground;[167] it is establish'd upon the Truth of that Being who is essential Truth it self, and is as surely his Word, as that there is a Heaven or an Earth, and as there is a Soul in Man.

At least be pleas'd to look back to what has been said in this Work to prove it, and observe that you cannot be certain it is not so, and if the Affirmative should prove really true, how fatal will your Mistake be?

> *If it should so fall out, as who can tell,*
> *But there may be a* GOD, *a* HEAVEN, *and* HELL,
> *Mankind had best consider well, for Fear*
> *'T should be too late when their Mistakes appear.*[168]

I appeal to general and common Understandings, whether it is a Matter to be cold and indifferent about, whether the Uncertainty is fit to be rested in, and to be easy under, whether the Consequence is not of Importance, and that sufficient to command your Attention?

To persuade you that there is a God, and that he cannot be just, that he is the Governour of the World, and yet that you may act according to the Gust of your own Desires,[169] without regard either to his Negative or Positive Commands; or rather that he has given you no Commands no Rules to walk by, but your own corrupted Reason, which is all one as to say, that he has set no Land-Marks upon your Conduct, no Bounds to your vilest Affections, prohibited nothing, and resents nothing; is this possible to reach your Understandings? is it not contrary to the Holiness and Righteousness of an infinitely pure Being? is it not repugnant to all the Principles of Government that have been learnt in the World? is it not repugnant to the very common Good of his Creatures? does not Reason shew it self too weak to be the sole Director of Mankind? does it not frequently stand still, nay perhaps sleep, while the worst of Crimes, taking the Reins of Government out of Reason's Hand, influences Mankind to ruin Kingdoms, destroy Nations, shed Rivers or rather Seas of Blood, and to practise all manner of publick and private Injuries?

How shall we reconcile these things to the Government of Reason! and how shall we reconcile the approving or not resenting these constant Injuries, Injustice, and Oppressions, to the Goodness of an infinitely gracious, clement, and beneficent Being? For God's sake, and for your own sakes, think again of these things, and you will soon be convinc'd, that certainly the righteous Hand of God, without the least Impeachment of his Goodness, is stretched out against such things,[170] and does reach the Heads of the Oppressors, either in this World or in another; indeed the Retribution not being always visible to us, and our prejudic'd Minds being eager to take all Advantages to support the wicked Insinuations of Error, we are apt to suggest that Heaven takes no notice of such things,[a] and to take a liberty, in our little Spheres, to do the like; according to that well known Text, *Eccl.* viii. 11. *Because sentence against an evil work is not executed speedily, therefore the heart of the sons of men is fully set in them to do Evil.*

But on the contrary, as the speedy Execution of Divine Justice, which is frequently exerted upon an evil Work, and upon the Workers of it also, is an undeniable Testimony of the Being of the Hand that executes it; so the Delay of that same Justice, which sometimes also happens, is as clear a Testimony of the Reality of a Future State and Judgment, and both are worth our Consideration; for if it was not a righteous Judge who acted in the *first Case*, the Blow would not have been given at all; and if it be a righteous Judge then, *in the second Case*, the Blow certainly remains to be given, and will fall, if not in this State in some other, that we cannot yet describe.

I need not look into History for Examples where the vindictive Attribute of God,[171] I mean his Anger and Vengeance against wicked Men, has been evidently stretched out in this Life, and when they have been punished in an awful and terrible manner; such things are recent in our Memory upon many sad Occasions: How can we then pretend that it is unworthy of God to resent the crying Sins of his Creatures? On the contrary, it would be repugnant to his Justice and Holiness not to do it.

In the next place, let those who incline to these Opinions, consider the Danger of running things up to such a dreadful Extremity; *who ever hardened himself against him and has prospered?*[172] Will any thinking Man venture to offend, because he thinks God will not punish, when there are Examples before his Eyes where God has punish'd, and has let loose his Anger upon others, and perhaps such as have been Offenders of a lower Degree than him that now presumes? are empty Notions and Suggestions sufficient to support the Mind against visible Testimonies of Fact?

Are not the daily Examples of the righteous Judgment of God, better Evidences of the Affirmative, than bare Suggestions of what *may be*, and as well *may not be*, are of the Negative? What think you of the Singularity of the vindictive Attribute, in so eminently pursuing the Guilt of Blood and bringing Murtherers to Justice? let it stand as a single Mark of the divine Vengeance, having not room to enlarge upon the many terrible Examples of other kinds which happen almost daily in our View. How does Hell haunt the guilty Soul, that he has no Rest Night or Day, till he even detects himself, and recognizes the divine Stroke of Justice in his own Destruction.

What shall we say to Publick Judgments by which God is pleased even to lay waste Nations, and unpeople whole Cities, nay Provinces, and Kingdoms? are they not Strokes of his Vengeance? if not why does not Almighty Sovereign Goodness interpose, to prevent those Calamities, and save his Creatures, for whom it is so eminently concern'd, and for whose Good all the Divine Attributes are so constantly employed?

Would the merciful God of Heaven, who is all Goodness and Beneficence, Pity, and Affection, to his Creatures, suffer them to be swept away in a Pestilence by thousands, as by an overflowing Stream;[173] and that even while they are on their Knees supplicating his infinite Goodness to spare them, if he did not think fit thus to testify his Resentment for their Offences, and to punish them for both their National and Personal Crimes? Can it be reconciled to his infinite Clemency, to desolate so many flourishing Kingdoms and Cities by War, Fire, Water, and other secondary Causes, which the Hand of his Goodness could easily restrain, if his Justice did not let them loose as Instruments of his Vengeance? How are Elements sometimes as it were armed against us? To day furious Lightnings destroy Men above Ground, to morrow terrible Earthquakes, bring subterraneous Judgments from below; to day violent Storms and Tempests overturn Cities and Towns; to morrow, dreadful Floods and Inundations of Rivers and Seas, sweep away thousands, and drown the whole Country: One while Rain is withheld, and the Earth is burnt up with Drought; another Season the Fruits of the Earth are destroy'd by continued and immoderate Rains.

To say these things have all their Causes in Order of Nature, and may be accounted for, is to say nothing; because, as you must acknowledge, the Power of God is infinitely able to restrain these Elements, and keep them from destroying his Creatures; where is his Almighty Sovereign Goodness, which is so exalted by this Principle of Deism, that it does not interpose to save his beloved Creatures? Why sleeps his protecting Providence, while the World is as it were brought to the Brink of the Precipice, and while his Creatures are perishing even within the Reach of his Pity?

Doubtless the Anger of God with-holds his Mercy on such Occasions as these, and he is punishing Men for their Transgressions, or else his Goodness would never suffer them to be thus overwhelmed with Ruin before his Face, while they had done nothing to provoke his Anger.

It is impossible to reconcile the publick Devastations, to the Goodness and Mercy of a being infinitely able to prevent them, if there were not Reasons to be drawn from his just Anger *against the Sins of Men, to account for them.*

Let these things be placed in the Balance, against all these modern Delusions; if the Soul is of Importance enough to move your Consideration, weigh them a little one against the other, and judge for yourselves whether it be consistent with your Reason, that while you believe there is a God, infinite, incomprehensible, and eternal, you can conceive so grossly of him as that he will make no Difference between the Righteous and the Wicked; that he will not distinguish the Wise, the Sober, the Just, and Upright, from the Profligate, the Vile, the Corrupt, and loose Livers; I say judge for your selves; let even that very Reason which you erect thus on the Throne of God judge for you, after which there is no more to be offered to you but this, with which I shall conclude.

Be a little Wary and Cautious; sit down sometimes and think what you are doing. Take heed how you make God your Jest, *how you mock at his Judgments,* and cast his Fear behind your Back;[174] least his Hand fall heavy upon you, least you come to recognize his Vengeance in your own Destruction, and implore his Mercy when it may be too late.

FINIS.

EXPLANATORY NOTES

1. *a Building fram'd in Heaven ... Jesus Christ himself is the chief corner Stone*: See Ephesians 2:19–21, where the 'household of God' is said to be 'built upon the foundation of the apostles and prophets, Jesus Christ himself being the chief corner stone. In whom all the building fitly framed together groweth unto an holy temple in the Lord'.

2. *Coup d'Eclat*: A *coup d'éclat* is 'a stroke which makes a sensation' (*OED* 5.l); used by Defoe in the *Review* (9 May 1706); *Letters Written by a Turkish Spy*, in *Satire, Fantasy and Writings on the Supernatural*, vol. 5, pp. 167, 151; *The Chimera: or, the French Way of Paying National Debts, laid Open* (1720), p. 55; *Minutes of the Negotiations of Mons. Mesnager* (1717), pp. 62, 140.

3. *they refuse him that speaketh from Heaven*: See Hebrews 12:25, 'See that ye refuse not him that speaketh. For if they escaped not who refused him that spake on earth, much more shall not we escape, if we turn away from him that speaketh from heaven'.

4. *Men are very fond of distinguishing themselves, not into good Principles but out of them*: In addition to the works cited on p. xiv above, see *Letters written by a Turkish Spy*, in *Satire, Fantasy and Writings on the Supernatural*, vol. 5, p. 117: 'Men may distinguish themselves into, and out of any Opinion or Religion in the World'.

5. *God ... created the Carcase of a Man*: See *OED* †2. *Obs.*, 'The living body considered in its material nature', i.e. not necessarily 'a term of contempt, ridicule, or indignity' (*OED* 3).

6. *breath'd ... a living Soul*: In Genesis 2:7, God 'breathed into his nostrils the breath of life; and man became a living soul'; repeated at p. 17 above.

7. *sensitive Life ... Brutes*: Here 'sensitive' means 'endowed with the faculty of sensation' (*OED* 2, citing Johnson's *Dictionary*, † 'Having sense or perception, but not reason'). Defoe frequently uses 'sensitive' in this obsolete sense, and draws the same distinction: see the *Compleat English Tradesman II*, in *Religious and Didactic Writings*, vol. 8, p. 125: 'STRANGE that the sensitive Life should enjoy a better Regimen than the Rational'; cf. *Jure Divino*, in *Satire, Fantasy and Writings on the Supernatural*, vol. 2, p. 130: 'Reason is the Gift that distinguishes Men from the Brutes; and 'tis observable that where a Man is depriv'd of the Use of his Reason, the sensitive Life that remains in him is less sagacious

than in the Common Brutes'. In the *Serious Reflections*, in *Novels*, vol. 3, p. 144, the sun is called 'the Giver of Life to all the Vegetative World ... enlivening and influencing the rational and sensitive Life'.

8. *inanimate*: Here the author goes on to gloss 'inanimate' as 'deprived of the Use of ... Reason, which is the Soul'; seven paragraphs later, he calls nature 'a meer Idiot, a demented inanimate Creature'. See 'A Vision of the Angelick World', in the *Serious Reflections*, in *Novels*, vol. 3, p. 256, where dogs and birds are called 'inanimate Creatures'. Defoe's usage is unusual but not unique; the '*Beasts and Cattle, and creeping Things*' of Psalm 148 are likewise referred to as 'Inanimate Creatures' by Simon Browne, in *God glorified by offering Praise. A Sermon* (1719), p. 16. See also *Mere Nature Delineated*, in *Writings on Travel, Discovery and History*, vol. 5, p. 156, for the phrase 'an inanimate Soul-less Form'. In all these passages 'inanimate' must mean 'without souls', which makes sense etymologically. Both *OED* definitions are patently inapplicable: '1. Not animated or alive; destitute of life, lifeless; *spec.* not endowed with animal life, as in *inanimate nature*, that part of nature which is without sensation, i.e. all outside the animal world. 2. Without the activity or motion of life (*lit.* and *fig.*); spiritless, inactive, dull'.

9. *occult Defect*: Here 'occult' means 'not detectable by the senses; imperceptible' (*OED* 2.b. *obs.*), or perhaps (as in medical usage) 'hidden, concealed, difficult to detect' (*OED* 3.c).

10. *to say ... is indeed to say nothing, or nothing to the Purpose*: see p. 36 above, 'To say ... is saying Nothing'; p. 61 above, 'To say ... is to say nothing'. In addition to the parallels cited at p. xiv above, see the Preface to *A Hymn to the Mob* (1715), in *Poetry*, in *Satire, Fantasy and Writings on the Supernatural*, vol. 1, p. 415: '*To say ... is to say nothing to the Purpose*'. Cf. also *Applebee's Journal*, 20 November 1725, in William Lee, *Daniel Defoe: His Life and Recently Discovered Writings*, 3 vols (1869), vol. 3, p. 443, 'To say ... is to say nothing to the Purpose'.

11. *Man of Nature ... without a Soul*: The thinking and the phraseology here resemble those Defoe had used apropos of the 'wild boy' recently brought over from Hanover, in *Mere Nature Delineated*; see *Writings on Travel, Discovery and History*, vol. 5, pp. 164–9.

12. *Discoveries and Improvements*: That the process of progressive revelation has yielded significant 'Discoveries and Improvements' beyond those originally vouchsafed to Adam in paradise parallels an argument that Defoe pursues in secular contexts, using these very terms: namely, that in such realms as science and technology, the advancement of knowledge owes as much or more to the ongoing development and application (i.e. the 'Improvement') of major inventions as to the inventions themselves (i.e. their 'Discovery'). This is a major theme of Defoe's *General History of Discoveries and Improvements*, in *Writings on Travel, Discovery and History*, vol. 4.

13. *Archimedes like*: The allusion is to the saying of the mathematician and physicist of the third century BC, that if he were given a place to stand he could move the world.

14. *Nature ... Ship without a Rudder*: For the same analogy, see *Mere Nature Delineated*, in *Writings on Travel, Discovery and History*, vol. 5, p. 169: the wild boy, 'in a State of MERE NATURE', acts 'just as Nature directs in other Creatures; but he is a Ship without a Rudder, not steer'd or managed, or directed by any Pilot'.

15. *the heavenly Vision*: See Acts 26:19, where St Paul tells Agrippa, 'I was not disobedient unto the heavenly vision'. In the *Serious Reflections*, in *Novels*, vol. 3, p. 193, Defoe says 'we are no Losers, if we observe the Rule laid down, *viz. That we be obedient to the heavenly Vision*'. Before the massacre on St Bartholomew's Day, Admiral Coligni neglected dreams and apparitions warning him of his danger, but others 'were more obedient to the heavenly Vision': see the *History and Reality of Apparitions*, in *Satire, Fantasy and Writings on the Supernatural*, vol. 8, p. 220. The verse is echoed again, p. 45 above.

16. *Igni fatui*: An *ignis fatuus* (Latin, 'foolish fire') popularly called a Will-o'-the-wisp, was 'a phosphorescent light seen hovering or flitting over marshy ground ... commonly used allusively or figuratively for any delusive guiding principle, hope, aim, etc'. (*OED*). See *A New Test of the Sence of the Nation* (1710), p. 9, in which '*Igni fatui*' are likened to 'Thoughts' that do not 'have any meaning at all' and are 'without any Signification'; here the notion of '*Natural Religion*' similarly has 'no significancy at all', but is pursued, as '*Igni fatui*' are, 'by Fools ... to their Destruction'. See also *Remarks on the Letter to the Author of the State-Memorial* (1706), p. 3, where Defoe says his adversaries 'amuse the Age with false Lights, the *Igni fatui*, of Abortive Envy, and Defeated Malice'. If in his known writings Defoe had always written the plural as '*igni fatui*', the fact that it appears in that form here might be construed as evidence of his authorship, or at any rate as a sign that the present work was not written by a divine, who would have been more likely to use the correct plural, '*ignes fatui*'. But '*Ignes fatui*' does appear in Defoe's writings at least once: see *Augusta Triumphans* (1728), in *Political and Economic Writings*, vol. 8, p. 283. The correct form of the singular ('*ignis fatuus*') occurs in *A Hymn to Victory* (1704), l. 638, in *Poetry*, in *Satire, Fantasy and Writings on the Supernatural*, vol. 1, p. 312; in the *Consolidator*, in *Satire, Fantasy and Writings on the Supernatural*, vol. 3, p. 158; in *Jure Divino*, bk 4, l. 117, in *Satire, Fantasy and Writings on the Supernatural*, vol. 2, p. 150; and in the *Complete English Tradesman I*, in *Religious and Didactic Writings*, vol. 7, p. 195.

17. *wholly brutal*: The *OED* labels *obs.* or *arch.* the meaning 'of or belonging to the brutes, as opposed to man; of the nature of a brute; animal', but Defoe often uses it in this sense: see *Robinson Crusoe*, in *Novels*, vol. 1, p. 125, 'Creatures, wild and tame, humane and brutal'; cf. *A System of Magick*, in *Satire, Fantasy and Writings on the Supernatural*, vol. 7, p. 36; *Plan of the English Commerce*, in *Political and Economic Writings*, vol. 7, p. 302.

18. *If Baal be a God ... since Men have thrown down his Altar*: See Judges 6:31 ('because one hath cast down his altar').

19. *if it is infinite in Prescience ... then Reason is GOD*: See the parallel passage from *A System of Magick* quoted on p. xiv above.

20. *Reason is erected ... into an Equality with Infinite, and is set up for a God*: for 'Infinite' as a noun, 'as a designation of the Deity or the absolute Being' (*OED* c.1), without modifier, see the *History and Reality of Apparitions, in Satire, Fantasy and Writings on the Supernatural*, vol. 8, p. 68: 'So that Infinite is not limited or ty'd up, to or from any degree of acting'; the *Commentator* (5 February 1720), in *Religious and Didactic Writings*, vol. 9, p. 57, where time is called 'the Child of Infinite'; *Mere Nature Delineated*, in *Writings on Travel, Discovery and History*, vol. 5, p. 205; and Adam hiding 'himself among a few Bushes from the search of, INFINITE', p. 26 above.

21. *whether will they go*: i.e. 'whither'.

22. *whether then will they fly?*: i.e. 'whither'.

23. *Lord Rochester ... Reason which fifty times for one does err*: See 'A Satyre Against Reason and Mankind', l. 11, in *The Works of John Wilmot Earl of Rochester*, ed. Harold Love (Oxford, 1998), p. 57; see citations of the *History and Reality of Apparitions* and the *Serious Reflections* at p. xv above.

24. *it is not in me*: The allusion is probably to Job's answer to the questions, 'where shall wisdom be found? and where is the place of understanding': 'The depth saith, It is not in me: and the sea saith, It is not with me' (Job 28: 12, 14). Joseph responds to Pharaoh with the same words (Genesis 41:16).

25. *Reason is frequently call'd an Emanation of Divine Light*: In *A System of Magick*, Defoe attacks the 'fine-spun Notions' of those who hold that reason is 'a Light issued from Heaven, and darted by Emanation into the Souls of Men': see *Satire, Fantasy and Writings on the Supernatural*, vol. 7, p. 153. Like the present work, *A System of Magick* attacks the view that 'the humane Judgment is in its self infallible, and therefore in some manner equal to the divine Being', and contends that "till God by Revelation directed it, all the Perfection of human Judgment could never lead Mankind to a right Knowledge of the Worship and Homage this Great Being requir'd'.

26. [Reason confesses] *that she knows but in part*: perhaps echoing 1 Corinthians 13:12, 'now we see through a glass, darkly ... now I know in part'.

27. *the God of Truth ... cannot lye*: See Titus 1:2, 'God, that cannot lie'.

28. *Nicodemus ... How can these things be?*: See John 3:9.

29. *Scripture is not allow'd ... yet we may bring Allusions from Scripture History*: See the parallel passages from three works by Defoe at p. xv above.

30. *a Maxim in Philosophy, That meer Matter cannot act upon immaterial Objects*: In the *Family Instructor II*, in *Religious and Didactic Writings*, vol. 2, p. 217, a father explains to his son that we know black people have souls 'because they exercise all the Faculties of the Soul', including an ability to

'act and operate upon immaterial Objects'. In *A System of Magick*, in *Satire, Fantasy and Writings on the Supernatural*, vol. 7, p. 216, Defoe says 'the Eyes of the Soul, which is a Spirit, can operate upon immaterial Objects, and see what to common Sight is call'd invisible'.

31. *the Natural Man cannot comprehend the things of God*: See 1 Corinthians 2:14 ('the natural man receiveth not the things of the Spirit of God').

32. *a Man of Learning, an Author of Fame, tell[s] us of the Religion of Nature*: The allusion is probably to [William Wollaston] (1659–1724), *The Religion of Nature Delineated* (1722), which went through several editions in the decade. Wollaston's title is echoed in Tindal's subtitle, *Christianity as Old as the Creation: or, the Gospel, a Republication of the Religion of Nature*.

33. *denominates*: to 'denominate' is 'to give (a thing) its name or character, to characterize; to make what it is, constitute' (*OED* 2.A, *obs.*); see the *Serious Reflections*, in *Novels*, vol. 3, p. 84, 'the Denomination of a Man's general Character'. In the *Review* (27 February 1705), truth is called man's '*Denominating Quality*'.

34. *distinguishes the brutal and sensitive Life*: Here 'sensitive' means 'endowed with the faculty of sensation' (*OED* 2a). See Defoe's note to book 3, l. 111 of *Jure Divino*, in *Satire, Fantasy and Writings on the Supernatural*, vol. 2, p. 130; *Conjugal Lewdness*, in *Religious and Didactic Writings*, vol. 5, p. 233; *Letters written by a Turkish spy*, in *Satire, Fantasy and Writings on the Supernatural*, vol. 5, p. 134; *Serious Reflections*, in *Novels*, vol. 3, p. 144; *Mere Nature Delineated*, in *Writings on Travel, Discovery and History*, vol. 5, p. 156; *A System of Magick*, in *Satire, Fantasy and Writings on the Supernatural*, vol. 7, p. 165.

35. *God, formed Man of the Dust of the Ground*: See Genesis 2:7.

36. *capable of acting upon Futurity, and upon Spirit, in a very extraordinary manner*: See the parallel passages from the *Serious Reflections* quoted at p. xv above.

37. *unsonorous*: The only eighteenth-century citation of 'unsonorous' in the *OED* is from *A Collection of Miscellany Letters, Selected out of Mist's Weekly Journal* (1722), vol. 1, p. 62, which contains a petition by 'You', 'Your', and other polite forms of address against the Quakers' 'Thee' and 'Thou': such locutions as '*Thee does*' are attacked as 'altogether unsonorous, and coarse in expressing, as well as incongruous in meaning'.

38. *speak it out, not knowing*: apparently not Scriptural, although italicized as if it were.

39. *Second Pastoral Letter ... publish'd just at the writing these Sheets*: See [Edmund Gibson (1669–1748)], *The Bishop of London's Second Pastoral Letter to the People of his Diocese ... Occasion'd by some Late Writings, in which it is asserted, That Reason is a sufficient Guide in Matters of Religion, without the Help of Revelation* (1730); the passage quoted is on p. 4. The *Second Pastoral Letter* came out within a week or two of Tindal's book: it is first advertised on 20 April 1730 in the *Daily Post*, which lists a second edition on 11 May and a third edition

on 29 May. It is not a reply to *Christianity as Old as the Creation*, but a general attack on Deism.

40. *all Exotic, receiv'd ... from a Power without herself*: Here 'Exotic' means 'drawn from outside; extrinsic' (*OED*, A.1.c., *obs.*, citing *A System of Magick*, in *Satire, Fantasy and Writings on the Supernatural*, vol. 7, p. 80, where mankind is 'under an absolute Necessity of some exotick Helps').

41. *Reason, says an old fashion'd Writer, is God's Candle in the Soul of Man*: 'an old fashion'd Writer' may be a jocular reference to Solomon; at any rate, this was the ordinary interpretation of Proverbs 20:27, 'The spirit of man is the candle of the LORD, searching all the inward parts of the belly'; see Poole, *Annotations*, on Job 25:3, n. f, 'The Light of Reason and Understanding, called God's Candle, Prov. 20. 27'. The image is a commonplace, used by John Locke, John Tillotson, Charles Morton and many others.

42. *unsignifying thing*: Defoe refers to 'unsignifying Dreams' in the *Serious Reflections*, in *Novels*, vol. 3, p. 232, and to 'unsignifying Significations' in *A System of Magick*, in *Satire, Fantasy, and Writings on the Supernatural*, vol. 7, p. 70.

43. *several farther Revelations ... in Paradise, and perhaps afterwards*: A key contention of the present work is that Christianity cannot be as old as creation because God's original revelation to Adam, although ample and sufficient for that time, had to be supplemented after the Fall by further revelations, among them the crucial promise (at the heart of Christianity) that man would be redeemed, and the breach between him and God healed, by the Messiah (see pp. 30–3 above). On the various senses in which a doctrine of 'progressive revelation' was understood and upheld in the early Eighteenth Century, see Jacob Viner, *The Role of Providence in the Social Order: An Essay in Intellectual History* (Princeton, NJ: Princeton University Press, 1972), p. 11; the actual term 'progressive revelation' occurs in the present work, p. 50 above.

44. *arrogant and assuming*: The *OED* defines the participial adjective 'assuming' as 'taking much upon oneself; taking for granted that one has a right to do so and so', but here the meaning is clearly 'presumptuous', as it is in *A General History of Discoveries and Improvements*, in *Writings on Travel, Discovery and History*, vol. 4, p. 123; in the *Compleat English Tradesman II*, in *Religious and Didactic Writings*, vol. 8, p. 222; and in *A Plan of the English Commerce*, in *Political and Economic Writings*, vol. 7, p. 122; cf. also 'too assuming for us to affirm', p. 7 above. Cf. Hogarth's 'No Dedication' to *The Analysis of Beauty*, 'Not dedicated to any man of quality for fear it might be thought too assuming'.

45. *fulness of Time*: See Galatians 4:4 ('fulness of time' in the Geneva, 'fulness of the time' in the Authorized Version); used again at p. 29 above.

46. *Phantosme*: here the meaning of phantom may be 'illusion, unreality; emptiness, vanity; delusion, deception, falsity', or perhaps 'an ineffectual ... thing; spec. one that has merely the title or outward appearance of power, authority, mastery, etc.; a cipher.' (*OED* 1a and 2b, both obsolete).

47. *Actings of the Soul ... prescrib'd, and narrow'd*: Here 'prescribe' means 'to limit, restrict, restrain; to confine within bounds' (*OED* 4). Defoe frequently couples 'narrow'd' and 'prescrib'd', e.g. *A New Family Instructor*, in *Religious and Didactic Writings*, vol. 3, p. 281; *The Advantages of Peace and Commerce; with some Remarks on the East-India Trade* (1729), p. 3.

48. *God cannot in justice require any name of us*: See *Christianity as Old as the Creation*: 'the Book of Nature shews us ... the Relation we stand in to God and our Fellow-Creatures, and the Duties resulting from thence ... then it must teach us the whole of our Duty, since it wou'd be unjust and tyrannical in any Being, to require more of others than the Relation they stand in to him makes it their Duty to pay' (432-page edn., p. 28; 391-page edn., p. 24). Tindal later maintains that it is 'evident from the Light of Nature, what are those Relations we stand in to God and our Fellow-Creatures; and that neither God nor Man, without acting tyrannically, can require more than Those require' (432-page edn., p. 70; 391-page edn., p. 59).

49. *the MESSIAH, which is, being interpreted, the CHRIST*: See John 1: 41.

50. *first Church ... erected at* Antioch: See Acts 11:20–6.

51. *as he says, we are ordered to examine the Truth of all the Gospel Revelation*: not an exact quotation from Tindal's *Christianity as old as the Creation*, but see 432-page edn. p. 186, 391-page edn. p. 164. The injunction to 'search the scriptures' occurs in John 5:39.

52. *guide us into all Truth*: See John 16:31, 'when he, the Spirit of truth, is come, he will guide you into all truth'.

53. *teach us all things, and bring all things to our remembrance*: See John 14:26, 'he shall teach you all things, and bring all things to your remembrance'.

54. *all the Light of Reason ... Revelation and nothing else*: See *A System of Magick*, in *Satire, Fantasy and Writings on the Supernatural*, vol. 7, p. 153: ''till God by Revelation directed it, all the Perfection of human Judgment could never lead Mankind to a right Knowledge of the Worship and Homage this Great Being requir'd ... unless GOD, the Author of all perfect and compleat Illumination, should add to it the Revelation of himself'.

55. *Cain ... not be accepted*: See Genesis 4:7.

56. *his first Fiat*: This seems to imply that there could be further fiats, a possibility alluded to in 'A Vision of the Angelick World', in the *Serious Reflections*, in *Novels*, vol. 3, p. 243, 'a new FIAT', i.e. a new act of creation, or a new divine command that there *be* a creation (the reference is to *fiat lux*, 'let there be light', in the Vulgate version of Genesis 1:3).

57. *imputed Righteousness*: In Reformed theology, this concept was an attempt to resolve the thorny problem of 'Justification' in a fallen world where 'perfect Obedience' is no longer possible, and where only 'the Merit of a Redeemer' suffices, not any worth of one's own. On this issue the Westminster Assembly's *Confession of Faith* is meticulous (Chap. 11, ¶ 1):

> Those whom God effectually calleth he also freely justifieth; not by infusing righteousness into them, but by ... accepting their persons as

righteous; not for any thing wrought in them, or done by them, but for
Christ's sake alone; not by imputing faith itself ... to them as their righteousness; but by imputing the obedience and satisfaction of Christ unto
them, they receiving and resting on him and his righteousness by faith:
which faith they have not of themselves; it is the gift of God.

58. *took a new Turn as we call it*: With '*as we call it*', Defoe often signals that a term
or phrase is idiomatic, colloquial, or (in the form 'as they call it') peculiar to a
regional dialect or occupational jargon. Examples abound in his works of the
1720s, e.g. *A Plan of the English Commerce*, in *Political and Economic Writings*,
vol. 7: 'overly, as we call it, and superficially' (p. 156); 'Scot and Lot, as we call
it' (p. 157); 'dragging, or as we call it, towing the boats' (p. 159); 'crowding too
much Sail, as the Seamen call it' (p. 184); the *History and Reality of Apparitions*,
in *Satire, Fantasy and Writings on the Supernatural*, vol. 8: a captain 'turn'd in
(as they call it at Sea) that is, went to Bed' (p. 189); a ship almost ran '*Bump
a-shore* (so the Sailors call it)' (p. 190). Such passages are especially frequent in
all three volumes of *A Tour thro' the Whole Island of Great Britain*, and versions
of 'took a new Turn' occur throughout Defoe's writings. See also p. 27 above,
'Cultivation, which we call to this day in some Dialects, labouring the Land'.

59. *our most horrid Excursions*: Here 'excursion' is used in the obsolete sense of 'a
deviation from custom, rule, or propriety' (*OED* 6.b).

60. *to hide himself among a few Bushes from the search of, INFINITE*: See the quotations from the *Political History of the Devil*, p. xvi above. In *Memoirs of the
Church of Scotland* (1717), in *Writings on Travel, Discovery and History*, vol. 6,
ed. N. H. Keeble (2002), p. 25, Defoe says that if ecclesiastical discipline were
as strict in England as in Scotland, errors and heresies could not be flaunted
openly: 'the Guilty would hide themselves, like *Adam*, among the Bushes'. In
both the Geneva and King James versions of Genesis 3:8, Adam and Eve hide
'amongst the trees', but Defoe's phrase is used by other Presbyterians. For Adam
hiding 'among the bushes', see T. Manton, *A Second Volume of Sermons* (1684),
p. 157. Matthew Henry quotes Genesis as 'amongst the trees', but comments
that 'In this Fright they *hid themselves* among the Bushes': see *An Exposition
of All the Books of the Old and New Testament*, 6 vols (1721–5), vol. 1, p. 15.

61. *to cover his Nakedness from the sight of Beasts*: See the quotation from the *Political History of the Devil*, p. xvi above; in Genesis 3:7, Adam and Eve 'sewed
fig leaves together, and made themselves aprons', but there is no indication of
motive, beyond the fact that 'they knew that they were naked': in other words,
there is no mention of avoiding 'the sight of Beasts'.

62. *here leaving the Scripture Account*: The author turns to a kind of historical
anthropology that features prominently in Defoe's writings, and that regularly
emphasizes the crudeness of religious thinking wherever people rely or have
relied on their own 'reason' rather than 'revelation'. The results, in his view,
have always and everywhere been 'the grossest Idolatries, and the vilest Corruptions' (p. 26 above). The Deists claimed that the pagans of antiquity and

the heathens in remote parts of the world have achieved religious wisdom; in Defoe's anti-Deist polemics, these achievements are challenged, e.g. by ridiculing the fabulous pantheon of Greco-Roman deities, and the empty pretensions of ancient oracles and soothsayers; by discrediting various belief systems found further afield and held up as exemplary by the Deists, such as those of the Incas and the Chinese; and by recounting the barbarities practiced by the Aztecs and other native Americans. Human sacrifice and cannibalism are brought forward as proof that left to himself, man is liable to degenerate into a brute. Moreover, even the wisest and best of the pagan moral philosophers, such as Socrates and Confucius, could not and did not arrive at the doctrinal 'truths' necessary to salvation, which (according to Defoe and other critics of Deism) only revelation afforded.

63. *Nulla gens tam barbara quæ nescit esse Deum*: In *Letters written by a Turkish Spy*, in *Satire, Fantasy and Writings on the Supernatural*, vol. 5, p. 117, Defoe quotes the full saying in the same words; in the *Serious Reflections*, in *Novels*, vol. 3, p. 151, he abbreviates it (see p. xvi above). See also G. Bull, *Some Important Points of Primitive Christianity Maintained and Defended*, 2nd edn, 3 vols (1714), vol. 3, p. 1081, '*nulla gens tam barbara, there is no Nation so barbarous ...* but that therein are to be found some Notions of a Deity'; cf. also Thomas Watson, *A Body of Practical Divinity* (1692), p. 21, '*Nulla gens tam barbara cui non insideat haec persuasio Deum esset*, Tully; No Nation so barbarous (saith Tully) as not to believe there is a God'. Although 'Tully' (Cicero) is usually cited as the source of this sentence, I have not found it in his writings.

64. *the Modus of his Worship*: Here 'modus' is 'the way in which something is done; a method, mode, or manner of operation. Now *rare*' (*OED* 5).

65. *as is preach'd in all the process of the Gospel*: Here 'process' is being used in the obsolete sense of 'the course or content of a narrative, treatise, argument, etc.; drift, tenor, gist' (*OED* 4.b).

66. *we call ... in some Dialects, labouring the Land*: 'Labouring the soil' occurs in *Paradise Lost* (Book 12, l. 18) and elsewhere, but by the eighteenth century to 'labour land', in the sense of tilling or cultivating it, seems to have become chiefly a Northern or Scottish idiom.

67. *in the sweat of his Brows*: See Genesis 3:19, 'In the sweat of thy face shalt thou eat bread'.

68. *Mr. Milton, with an admirable Turn of Invention*: See Michael's speech to Adam in *Paradise Lost*, Book 11, ll. 423f.

69. *as Types of the great Attonement*: see also 'Types were to cease, and be swallow'd up in the thing typified', p. 37 above]): in its theological sense, a 'type' is 'a person, object, or event of Old Testament history, prefiguring some person or thing revealed in the new dispensation' (*OED* 1.a).

70. *a Lamb, or firstling as 'tis call'd*: See Genesis 4:4.

71. *burning them to God*: In Genesis 4 there is no mention of '*burning*' Cain's or Abel's 'offerings'; the earliest instance of sacrificial objects (in this case animals) being burned is in the Noah story, Genesis 8.

72. *as a Quit-Rent for the Tenure of the Lands they held*: Quit-rent is a 'small Acknowledgment paid in Money, so call'd because such Payment did acquit the Tenant from all other Service or Duties to the Lord' (J. Cowell, *A Law Dictionary*, 1708); or alternatively '*quasi Quiet-Rent*', or 'a certain small Rent, payable yearly by the Tenants of most Manors, in Token of Subjection; which, when paid, the Tenant is *quiet* and free till it becomes due again' (T. Blount, *A Law-Dictionary*, 3rd edn, 1717). In the present passage the term is used figuratively, as it is by Defoe in the *Family Instructor II*, in *Religious and Didactic Writings*, vol. 2, p.108, and in the *Serious Reflections*, in *Novels*, vol. 3, p. 69.

73. *a reasonable Service*: See Romans 12:1, where St. Paul urges 'that ye present your bodies a living sacrifice, holy, acceptable unto God, which is your reasonable service'.

74. *Heb. xi 4*: The actual reading of Hebrews 11: 4 is 'Abel offered unto God a more excellent sacrifice than Cain'; probably quoting from memory, Defoe evidently recalled all the other references to 'acceptable' sacrifices, e.g. Rom. 12:1; Philippians 4:18; 1 Peter 2:5.

75. *the Fruit of their Bodies, for the Sin of their Souls*: See Micah 6:7, 'shall I give my firstborn for my transgression, the fruit of my body for the sin of my soul?' Cf. the *Family Instructor I*, in *Religious and Didactic Writings*, vol. 1, p. 81; repeated at p. 37 above.

76. *But let us keep where we are*: i.e. stay with the subject, rather than digressing into a survey of 'the grossest Absurdities' (p. 35 above) that the pagan world has descended to in its customs of worship – a topic explored at length in the *Serious Reflections* and the *Political History of the Devil*, in both of which a more crucial role is assigned to the Devil than to the weakness of unaided human reason.

77. *How incongruous was the very thing call'd a Sacrifice, or Burnt-Offering*: This sense of incongruity is not merely a modern reaction, but is already signalled in Scriptural passages such as Psalm 50:8–13:

> I will not reprove thee for thy sacrifices or thy burnt offerings, to have been continually before me. I will take no bullock out of thy house, nor he goats out of thy folds. For every beast of the forest is mine, and the cattle upon a thousand hills. I know all the fowls of the mountains: and the wild beasts of the field are mine. If I were hungry, I would not tell thee: for the world is mine, and the fulness thereof. Will I eat the flesh of bulls, or drink the blood of goats?

Burnt offerings occur in the earlier stories of Noah and of Abraham and Isaac (Genesis 8, 22), and are explicitly linked with sacrifices in Exodus and later books, but this Psalm brings out most clearly and ironically 'how incongruous' it is to sacrifice animals to a deity conceived of in spiritual rather than physical terms, and who is both creator and possessor of everything man sacrifices to him.

In demanding (two paragraphs earlier) 'Where was the sense of it', the present author faces the kind of Old Testament problem the Deists made much of. He regards such anomalies as evidence that there must have been 'a subsequent Communication of the Mind and Will of God to Mankind' by means of post-Edenic revelation. The Deists, on the contrary, see them as casting doubt on the authenticity of any revelation so 'incongruous' with 'reasonable Thoughts' about religion or the deity, and ultimately on the validity of revelation itself.

78. *an immediate Intelligence with*: Here 'Intelligence' is used in the obsolete sense of 'interchange of knowledge, information, or sentiment; mutual conveyance of information; communication, intercourse' (*OED* 5.a).

79. *the Life and Light of the World*: See John 8:12, 9:5, 6:51.

80. *shall not perish, but have ever-lasting Life*: See John 3:16.

81. *the Way, and the Truth, and the Life ... but by him*: See John 14:6, 'I am the way, the truth, and the life: no man cometh unto the Father, but by me'.

82. *in the first Ages of Time, so call'd the Beginning of Time*: Although italicized as if it were a Biblical citation, the phrase '*Beginning of Time*' does not occur in Scripture, where 'the beginning of the world' is common in both the Old and the New Testament. However, Defoe may simply be thinking of Genesis 1, 'In the beginning...'.

83. *Servants of this Jesus were called Christians*: See Acts 11:26, 'the disciples were called Christians first in Antioch'.

84. *Death by Sin*: See Romans 5:12, 'by one man sin entered into the world, and death by sin'.

85. *no Sin ... no Expiation ... not offended ... no Propitiation*: Related but distinct theological terms, 'Expiation' is something done to remove or make up for the guilt of sin itself, while 'Propitiation' is something done to appease or conciliate God, 'offended' by sin; in atoning for sinful mankind, Christ combines both functions. Ephraim Chambers defines 'expiation' as 'the Act of *Suffering* the Punishments adjudged to a Man's Crimes, and thus paying off and discharging the Guilt', and 'propitiation' as 'a Sacrifice offer'd to God to assuage his Wrath, and render him propitious': see *Cyclopædia: or, an Universal Dictionary of Arts and Sciences*, 2 vols (1728), vol. 1, p. 168, vol. 2, p. 894.

86. *no Christ, and consequently no Christianity*: The meaning is not that Christ did not yet exist, but merely that there was no occasion for him to take on his role as man's redeemer until Adam had fallen. This is expressed more clearly at pp. 40–1 above: 'there was a time when [Christianity] was not, when the Doctrine of a Christ, or a Redeemer was *not*; that is to say, was not heard of, was not wanted'.

87. *as needless as it is impossible to know*: In *Letters written by a Turkish Spy*, in *Satire, Fantasy and Writings on The Supernatural*, vol. 5, p. 126, Mahmut says, 'How this is perform'd ... is as needless as it is impossible to know'; see also the

passages from the *Review* and the *Political History of the Devil* quoted on p. xvi above.

88. *Christianity ... not an innate Idea*: The supposition that certain ideas are inborn had been challenged by Locke's *Essay concerning Humane Understanding* (1690), which maintained that all our ideas are obtained through the mind operating on sense-experience.

89. *So that ... the Fall of Man*: The principle enunciated in this and the surrounding paragraphs, that in effect Christianity dates from the moment of God's speech to Adam in Genesis 3:15, is summarized in a section of the Westminster Assembly's *Confession of Faith* (1649 and many later editions),'Of Christ the Mediator', Chap. 8, ¶ 6: 'Although the work of redemption was not actually wrought by Christ till after his incarnation, yet the virtue, efficacy, and benefits thereof, were communicated unto the elect in all ages successively from the beginning of the world, in and by those promises, types, and sacrifices, wherein he was revealed and signified to be the Seed of the woman, which should bruise the serpent's head'.

90. *Mr. Calvin, in his Institutions*: The reference is apparently to book 2, ch. 6 of the *Institutes of the Christian Religion* of Jean Calvin (1509–64), a key document of Reformation theology, published in Latin and French editions during Calvin's lifetime, and in numerous Sixteenth- and Seventeenth-Century English editions and abridgments, usually entitled *Institution* but sometimes (as here) *Institutions*.

91. *the Salvation, and the Consolation of Israel*: References to the salvation of Israel in the Psalms and elsewhere were interpreted as anticipations of Christ's redemptive role; the consolation of Israel and salvation through Christ are linked in the story of Simeon, Luke 2:25–32, mentioned four paragraphs earlier.

92. *Adam might well have reply'd to God himself, What occasion have I for all this?*: I.e., if Adam had not offended, there would have been no need of the 'Doctrine of Salvation' or 'Notions of Redemption'. Here, however, the manner of Adam's challenge is of greater interest than its substance: to impute such brashness to him seems very like Defoe, who regularly treats Biblical characters, actions and speeches facetiously, and even irreverently, yet not (in my opinion) sceptically. The notion that anything short of sanctimonious solemnity implies disbelief is as alien to Defoe as to the author of *A Tale of a Tub*. Cf. *Serious Reflections,* in *Novels*, vol. 3, p. 201: 'we hope God will not *put us off* SO'.

93. *inverting the Order of things*: See *The Great Law of Subordination consider'd*, in *Religious and Didactic Writings*, vol. 6, ed. J. A. Downie (2007), p. 97, where Defoe says the poor enjoy so many privileges in England that 'they bid fair for inverting the Order of things'.

94. *MANY learned Men ... he would be best pleased*: This paragraph corresponds with the father's summary of his 'Thoughts about Religion' in *A New Family Instructor*, in *Religious and Didactic Writings*, vol. 3, p. 59, 60: 'The Belief of the

Being *of a God* is the first Principle; 'tis the first Truth Nature dictates: That a
Homage is due to that *God* ... is the next. The Manner how that Homage is to
be paid, is the third; and this we call Religion'. He goes on to explain that 'our
Debt and Duty' is to 'pay that Homage ...... in such a Manner as is agreeable to
his revealed Word and Will'. More broadly, it follows the principles laid down
in the *Confession of Faith* of the Westminster Assembly of Divines, Chap. 21,
¶ 1, '*Of Religious Worship*': 'The light of Nature sheweth that there is a GOD',
who is to be 'feared, loved, praised, called upon, trusted in, and served'. 'But, the
acceptable way of worshipping the true God', it continues, 'is instituted by himself, and so limited by his own revealed Will, that he may not be worshipped
according to the imaginations and devises of men ... or any other way not pre-
scribed in the holy Scripture'.

95. *God whose Wisdom is unsearchable, and his Ways past finding out*: See Romans
   11:33, 'O the depth of the riches both of the wisdom and knowledge of God!
   how unsearchable are his judgments, and his ways past finding out!'

96. *under the Sentence of THE DEATH, as it is emphatically exprest*: See Matthew
   15:4, Mark 7:10.

97. *opinionative and conceited*: 'Holding obstinately to one's own opinion; opinionated' (*OED*); Defoe uses 'opinionative', 'opinionated' and '*opinionatre*',
   sometimes associating this trait with conceit: thus the Portuguese pilot Crusoe meets in China is very 'opinionated and conceited' (*Farther Adventures*,
   in *Novels*, vol. 2, p. 160), and Roxana's first husband is 'a conceited Fool, *Tout
   Opinionatre*' (*Fortunate Mistress*, in *Novels*, vol. 9, p. 26). Cf. also *Compleat
   English Gentleman*, in *Religious and Didactic Writings*, vol. 10, pp. 162, 164;
   the *Serious Reflections*, in *Novels*, vol. 3, p. 260.

98. *Doctrine of a Satisfaction*: On this doctrine, see the passage from the Westminster Assembly *Confession of Faith* (Chap. 11, ¶ 1) quoted above, n. 57.
   Satisfaction has a specific meaning in Calvinist theology: Christ 'satisfies'
   divine justice by taking the punishment mankind deserves upon himself. The
   author goes on to explain and support the related concepts of 'Propitiation for
   their Guilt' and 'propitiatory Sacrifice' on the next two pages; on expiation and
   propitiation, see also n. 85 above.

99. *thousands of Rams, and Ten thousands of Rivers of Oil*: See Micah 6:7, 'Will the
   LORD be pleased with thousands of rams, or with ten thousands of rivers of
   oil?'; the words that follow, from the end of the verse, are quoted above, p. 28.

100. *In the Crisis of this Exigence*: Here 'Exigence', rather than being a redundant
   term for crisis, probably means 'A pressing state of circumstances, or one
   demanding immediate action or remedy; a difficulty, extremity, strait' (*OED*
   2, citing *Political History of the Devil*, in *Satire, Fantasy and Writings on the
   Supernatural*, vol. 6, p. 145).

101. *as King Charles the Second said*: A possible source for this saying is *Bishop
   [Gilbert] Burnet's History Of his own time*, 3 vols (1725), vol. 2, p. 608: 'Some
   things he [King Charles] freely condemned, such as living with another man's

wife: Other things he excused, and thought God would not damn a man for a little irregular pleasure'.

102. exalted above all his Name: See Nehemiah 9:5, 'Stand up and bless the LORD your God for ever and ever: and blessed be thy glorious name, which is exalted above all blessing and praise'.

103. *when he said, I was afraid*: See Genesis 3:10.

104. *decreed it, tho' ... not unalterably*: Belief in predestination, one of the most controversial doctrines of Calvinism, lost ground considerably after the Restoration; the traditional position is expressed in the Westminster Assembly's *Confession of Faith*, 'Of God's Eternal Decree', but the present passage may be commenting ironically on the notion that God has 'unchangeably ordain[ed] whatsoever comes to pass' (Chap. 3, ¶ 1).

105. *This Mr. Milton represents in a most sublime Light*: See *Paradise Lost*, Book 11, ll. 22–44.

106. *one and only Mediator ... Christ Jesus*: See 1 Timothy 2: 5.

107. *hold up his Hand, as we might call it*: Adam is challenged as if he were a defendant in court, who was required to raise his hand to be sworn: see the *History and Reality of Apparitions*, in *Satire, Fantasy and Writings on the Supernatural*, vol. 8, p. 113, 'When he came to hold up his Hand at the Bar, he pleaded, *Not Guilty*'.

108. *talk'd like a Fool*: See the parallel passages from the *Political History of the Devil* quoted on p. xvi above.

109. *she gave it me*: See Genesis 3:12.

110. *the Serpent beguiled me*: See Genesis 3:13.

111. *genuine History of the Fact; whether in Allegory or not, is not material to the Case*: How any story – not just the Biblical account of the fall – could be at once historical *and* allegorical has been a source of perplexity for commentators on Defoe. Unlike modern critics, who see the genres of history and allegory as mutually exclusive if not opposed, Defoe seems to regard them as coexisting within works such as *Robinson Crusoe*, which he represents in the *Serious Reflections*, in *Novels*, vol. 3, p. 126, as having been an 'allusive allegorick History'. On these matters see Brian Cummings, 'Protestant Allegory', in the *Cambridge Companion to Allegory*, ed. Rita Copeland and Peter T. Struck (Cambridge: Cambridge University Press), 2010, pp. 177–90.

112. *by one Man ... from the Curse*: See Romans 5:12; 1 Timothy 2:5; Galatians 3:13.

113. *with Epicurus ... to deny that there was any first Man at all ... the Doctrine of the Eternity of the World*: Defoe usually represents Epicurus as holding that the world came into existence randomly, not that it had always existed. See the *Serious Reflections*, in *Novels*, vol. 3, p. 116: '*Epicurus* ... fancies the World was made by a Strange fortuitous Conjunction of Atoms'; in *Letters Written by a Turkish Spy*, in *Satire, Fantasy and Writings on the Supernatural*, vol. 5, p. 186, Defoe refers to 'the old Notion of *Epicurus*, that the World was made, or rather made it self, by meer Chance, by a fortuitous Conjunction of Atoms';

cf. also his mocking reference in the *Review* (25 June 1706) to 'Epicurus's *for-tuitous Atoms, which they say, form'd the World*'. Archbishop Tillotson says, 'the Heathens did generally acknowledge the making of the World, and the Pres-ervation and Government of it' to be the work of a divinity, but he qualifies this by adding, 'except *Aristotle*, who supposed the World not to have been made, but to have been from Eternity; and *Epicurus* with his Followers, who ascribed the regular and orderly Frame of Nature to a happy casualty and for-tunate concourse of Atoms': see *The Remaining Discourses, on the Attributes of God*, ed. R. Barker, 3rd edn (1704), vol. 7, pp. 289 [misnumbered 293]–90. Sir Richard Blackmore treats '*The Absurdity of asserting the Self-existent, Inde-pendent and Eternal Being of Atomes according to the Scheme of* Epicurus' in Book 3 of *Creation. A Philosophical Poem* (1712), 'The Argument', p. 105; and Defoe repeatedly challenges 'Notions of the World's Eternity' (*Letters Written by a Turkish Spy*, p. 187) by asserting that '*some Power must first bestow / Exist-ence on those Atoms*' whose random convergence, according to the Epicureans, '*form'd the World*'.

114. *a Notion too gross to deserve a Reply, and too ridiculous to bring it into a Discourse so solemn and serious*: In *Letters written by a Turkish Spy*, in *Satire, Fantasy and Writings on the Supernatural*, vol. 5, pp. 186–7, Defoe declares that the phi-losophers 'in this Nation of Atheists and Deists' who 'follow the old Notion of *Epicurus*', argue 'not only absurdly, but even to the last Degree weakly and fool-ishly', particularly in holding a view 'of Man being his own Maker': if that were so, '*Man must be eternal*; for what could give it self Life, could certainly preserve Life; and if Man is eternal, then Man is God; for whatever is eternal is God'. In *A System of Magick*, in *Satire, Fantasy and Writings on the Supernatural*, vol. 7, p. 183, he is similarly contemptuous of the '*Weakness, Ignorance, and* Emptyness' of a scheme that postulates '*A* self-deriving *World, a* self-creating *Man*'. In that work, instead of tracing its classical sources, he associates this doctrine with the 'wild Philosophy' propagated by atheistic moderns: '*How do the Naturalists, and* [Royal Society] SO SO's *Dream*' when they try to explain '*a* Nature *void of* GOD'.

115. *Legion ... enter into the Herd*: In Luke 8:27–33, Christ allows devils to leave a man and enter a herd of swine. This is a very peculiar (and unorthodox) meta-phor for the etiology of sin, but Defoe was partial to far-fetched applications of this text. In *A Hymn to the Mob* (1715), ll. 616–53, a '*MOB* posses'd with *Party-Spleen, / Is like the Devil* in the Herd of Swine'; see *Poetry*, in *Satire, Fantasy and Writings on the Supernatural*, vol. 1, pp. 434–5, and the editor's remarks on 'Defoe's habitual tendency towards facetiousness when discussing Bible sto-ries', Introduction, p. 34. Defoe draws on the versions in Matthew 8:28–33 and Mark 5:2–13 as well as that of Luke for various purposes, often playful or satirical, in *Jure Divino*, bk 5, ll. 735–7, in *Satire, Fantasy and Writings on the Supernatural*, vol. 2, p. 197; the *Political History of the Devil*, in *Satire, Fantasy and Writings on the Supernatural*, vol. 6, pp. 99, 157, 261, 271, 276, 284; *A System of Magick*, in *Satire, Fantasy and Writings on the Supernatural*, vol. 7, p.

270; the *History and Reality of Apparitions*, in *Satire, Fantasy and Writings on the Supernatural*, vol. 8, p. 96; *A New Family Instructor*, in *Religious and Didactic Writings*, vol. 3, p. 285. In any case, Defoe was fascinated by this episode, and his hardy treatment of it shows amusingly that his deference to Scripture, which was genuine and profound, was by no means slavish.

116. *Death passed ... all have sinned*: See Romans 5:12.

117. *a Golden Age ... the Iron Age*: In classical mythology, eras corresponding with the Judaeo-Christian images of Edenic peace and abundance and later strife and hardship; thus an originally 'glorious State of Things' got 'overthrown and reduc'd' through processes of degeneration analogous to Adam's.

118. *the original Propensity to offend*: In the *Family Instructor I*, in *Religious and Didactic Writings*, vol. 1, Defoe speaks of 'a natural Propensity we all have to Evil' (p. 90), 'a Natural Propensity in us to do evil, and no Natural Inclination to do Good' (p. 59), and 'the perverse and wicked Inclinations' of children (p. 70); in 'A Vision of the Angelick World', in the *Serious Reflections*, in *Novels*, vol. 3, p. 228, he speaks of 'our Propensity to Evil rather than Good' being 'a Testimony of the original Depravity of human Nature'. Early in his career, in *A New Discovery of an Old Intreague* (1691), ll.61–4, in *Poetry*, in *Satire, Fantasy and Writings on the Supernatural*, vol. 1, p. 51, he had written, 'So swift are Men to desperate Ills design'd, / To ill spontaneous, and in good confin'd. A proof the evil Principle is first, / And Guilt has all the Power to Will engross'd'. See also p. 21 above, 'the propensity in the Will of Man to offend'.

119. *Who is so merciful, he can't be just*: See the parallels from *A New Family Instructor*, the *Serious Reflections*, and *A System of Magick* quoted on p. xvi above.

120. *the wrath of God ... unrighteousness*: Defoe cites the same verse in *A New Family Instructor*, in *Religious and Didactic Writings*, vol. 3, p. 205, as part of a similar argument that God is 'angry, and will ... deal in the utmost Vengeance and Resentment against the guilty Sinner, unless he repents', as against the Deist view that God looks on sinners 'with Pity indeed and Compassion, but no Anger and Displeasure, which is below his Infinite Greatness, and the Sovereignty of his Mercy'.

121. *no Atonement without a Sacrifice, no Sacrifice without a Priest, no Priest without an Altar, no Altar without a mercy Seat*: This figure of speech (isocolon) occurs frequently in Defoe's works, usually coupled with paradox or oxymoron. See his 'Historicall Collections' (1682), listing 'twelve Absurdities' from a treatise by St Cyprian 'of the life of man': '1 A wise man without good works. 2 An old man without Religion. 3 A young man w:thout Obedience. 4 A Rich man without Almes. 5 A Guide without vertue'. In *The Consolidator*, in *Satire, Fantasy and Writings on the Supernatural*, vol. 3, p. 58, Defoe says, 'Here was Plunder without *Violence*, Violence without *Persecution*, Conscience without *Good Works*, and Good Works without *Charity*'. See *A General History of Discoveries and Improvements*, in *Writings on Travel, Discovery and History*, vol. 4, pp. 175–6, a long catalogue that begins, 'THEY had *Philosophy* without Experiment. *MATHEMATICKS* without Instruments. *GEOGRAPHY*

without Scale. *ASTRONOMY* without Demonstration' and so on. In a poem prefixed to vol. 8 of the *Review* (1712), pp. 9–10, Defoe says, 'I'm pleas'd *without Impertinence*, / And Angry *without Sin*. / Thoughtful without Anxiety, / And griev'd *without* Despair; / Chearful, *but without* Levity, / And cautious *without* fear'. In the *Compleat English Tradesman II*, in *Religious and Didactic Writings*, vol. 8, p. 115, he says of slander, "tis a Thunder without a Bolt, a Cannon fir'd without a Ball, Rage without a Weapon, a Snake without a Sting'. See *Serious Reflections*, in *Novels*, vol. 3, p. 148: religion in Italy is said to consist of 'Meditation without Worship, Doctrine without Practice, Reflection without Reformation, and Zeal without Knowledge'. In *Religious Courtship*, in *Religious and Didactic Writings*, vol. 4, p. 66, conversation having nothing to do with religion is 'like a Dance without Musick, a Song without Measure; like Poetry without Quantity, or Speech without Grammar'. In *Mere Nature Delineated*, in *Writings on Travel, Discovery and History*, vol. 5, p. 204, Defoe describes a cheerful fool who 'raves without Passion, blasphemes without Prophaneness, Curses without Malice, Drinks without Taste, Sings without Musick, and Talks without Sense'. In *A System of Magick*, in *Satire, Fantasy and Writings on the Supernatural*, vol. 7, pp. 241–2, Defoe contrasts former times, in which men 'had the Sublime without the Infernal, the Humid without the Horrid ... the Fire without the Brimstone; they could laugh without Baudy, and jest without Blasphemy; talk without Buffoonry, and vote without Bribery; write without Pedantry, and read without Party', with the present, in which 'we laugh without a Jest, and jest without Wit; we write without Sense, and read without Taste ... we preach without Doctrine, are religious without Principles; pray without Doxology, and worship without a God'.

122. *the everlasting Gospel*: See Revelation 14:6.
123. *Scripture ... none but God could know*: See *A New Family Instructor*, in *Religious and Didactic Writings*, vol. 3, pp. 212–3, 216–17, where the first argument that Scripture 'must be *the Word of God*' is that 'It has reveal'd what none but GOD could know'. The father's recital of many Biblical prophecies and their fulfilment leads his daughter to exclaim, 'Indeed these Things do not look as if Man could reveal and discover them'.
124. *the whole Body of the New Testament History, is a Testimonial of their* [viz. 'Old Testament Promises and Prophecies'] *being punctually fulfill'd*: See *A New Family Instructor*, in *Religious and Didactic Writings*, vol. 3, p. 208, where one of the features of Scripture which 'prove it to be the Word of GOD' is that 'all its Prophecies, of which it is so full, whose appointed Time has been come, have been punctually and exactly accomplish'd'; cf. also p. 246, where 'not one Tittle of all that had been foretold' failed 'to come exactly and punctually to pass'.
125. *It is a faithful saying, and worthy of all acceptation*: 1 Timothy 1:15 actually reads, 'This is a faithful saying, and worthy of all acceptation, that Christ Jesus came into the world to save sinners; of whom I am chief'; the present passage treats '*It*' as if its antecedent were Scripture itself.

126. *there are some Difficulties in the reading ... in their Minds*: See *A New Family Instructor*, in *Religious and Didactic Writings*, vol. 3, p. 267, where the father criticizes unbelievers who, 'leaving the plain and undeniable Consequences of Things, and turning or wresting the Scriptures to their own particular Meanings, would ... seek for Shifts and Subterfuges in the different Readings, and doubtful ambiguous Construction of Words to avoid the Force of plain and pungent Texts; so to lessen the Credit of them, or leave us unsatisfied of the true Sense, till they can decide those jarring Disputes, reconcile those Readings, and have all their Objections answered and silenced, which may probably never be brought to pass'.

127. *the very Image of God stampt upon every part ... a visible Signature of the Divine Authority*: See also 'eminent Signatures of the high Original of the Scriptures', p. 48 above, and the very similar passage from *A New Family Instructor* quoted on p. xiii above.

128. *would bewray its Author by its Imperfections*: To 'bewray' is 'To reveal, expose, discover ... the true character of' (*OED* 6.b, *arch.*).

129. GOD *of* TRUTH: See Deuteronomy 32:4, Psalm 31:5.

130. *a wonderful Concurrence of Circumstance*: See the *Review* passages quoted on p. xvii above.

131. *the promis'd Deliverances arriv'd ... the self-same Day, says the Text*: See *A New Family Instructor*, in *Religious and Didactic Works*, vol. 3, p. 210: the prophecy regarding 'the Bondage of the *Israelites* in *Egypt*' was 'fulfilled even to a Day, *the self-same Day*, Exod. xii.17, 51'.

132. *Threatned Deluge, long before ... Gen. vii. 4*: See *A New Family Instructor*, in *Religious and Didactic Works*, vol. 3, p. 210: 'the drowning of the World ... was revealed to *Noah* ... 120 Years before its Accomplishment ... and again, God foretels it to *Noah* just a Week before it was to happen, *Gen.* vii. 4. and accordingly it did happen'.

133. *casting down Jeroboam's Altar ... Josiah ... fulfill'd*: See 1 Kings 13.

134. *the destruction of Jerusalem, and the captivity in Babylon ... most exactly fulfill'd*: These prophecies and their fulfilment are discussed in similar terms – that is, as confirming 'the Divine Authority and Original of the Scripture' – in *A New Family Instructor*, in *Religious and Didactic Works*, vol. 3, pp. 210–11.

135. *the Devil, whose Power of Prediction, some have suggested to be great, tho' there is nothing of that kind in his Power*: See the passages from *A New Family Instructor*, the *History and Reality of Apparitions*, the *Political History of the Devil*, and *A System of Magick* cited on p. xvii above.

136. *Are not these marks of a Divine Impression?*: See the parallel passage from *A New Family Instructor* cited on p. xiii above.

137. *if it had*: The sense seems to require 'if it had *been* unworthy or inconsistent ...'.

138. *Scripture ... a perfect rule of Life ... to his own eternal Felicity ... to be receiv'd with ... an intire Credence*: With these two paragraphs, compare *A New Family Instructor*, in *Religious and Didactic Works*, vol. 3, p. 216: if Scripture is really

the 'Word of GOD', 'then an intire Belief of it is just and reasonable, and is our indispensable Duty: It is to be credited in every thing it says ... 'tis to be receiv'd, as indeed it is, the Word of Life, the Voice of GOD, ... and containing in it a compleat Rule of Life, with every thing needful to our eternal Felicity'. Cf. also the *Confession of Faith* of the Westminster Assembly of Divines, which begins with a chapter 'Of the Holy Scripture' (Chap. 1, ¶ 1, 4):

Although the Light of Nature, and the Works of Creation and Providence ... manifest the Goodness, Wisdom, and Power of God ... yet they are not sufficient to give that Knowledge of God and of His Will, which is necessary unto Salvation. Therefore it pleased the Lord, at sundry times, and in divers manners, to reveal himself, and to declare that His Will unto His Church; and afterwards ... to commit the same wholly unto Writing: which maketh the Holy Scripture to be most necessary ... ¶ The Authority of the Holy Scripture, for which it ought to be believed and obeyed, dependeth ... wholly upon God (who is Truth it self) the Author thereof; and therefore it is to be received, because it is the Word of God.

139. the *Affirmative is reasonable, the Negative only presumptive*: See *The Experiment: Or, The Shortest Way with the Dissenters Exemplified. Being the Case of Mr. Abraham Gill* (1705), p. 5: 'a sight of the Originals is but a presumptive Proof'. Cf. also *Remarks on the Letter to the Author of the State-Memorial* (1706), p. 14: 'that this Occult Project was true, is very uncertain, and the Suggestion very presumptive, as it is really very improbable'. The closest *OED* definition of 'presumptive' – 'Based on presumption or inference; presumed, inferred' (3.a) – fails to convey the doubtfulness in these passages; Phillips's contemporary definitions of 'To Presume' as 'to imagine, think, conjecture, or suppose', and of 'Presumption' as 'Conjecture, Guess, Suspicion', seem nearer the mark.

140. *on which side lies the hazard? ... in the greatest imaginable Risque*: See above, pp. xxix–xxx and n. 35.; Defoe's version of the Pascalian wager is adapted from the *Pensées* (1670), translated as *Monsieur Pascall's Thoughts, Meditations, and Prayers, Touching Matters Moral and Divine* (1688), pp. 74–6, and as *Thoughts on Religion, and Other Subjects* (1704), pp. 59–60.

141. *Books of the Sybils, the Oracles of the Heathen, and the Conjurations of the Magicians*: On 'Magick and Conjurations', see the *History and Reality of Apparitions*, in *Satire, Fantasy and Writings on the Supernatural*, vol. 8, p. 82; on the heathen oracles, whom Defoe regards as 'Cheats and Imposters', see the *Political History of the Devil*, in *Satire, Fantasy, and Writings on the Supernatural*, vol. 6, pp. 187–92; cf. also *A System of Magick*, in *Satire, Fantasy and Writings on the Supernatural*, vol. 7, p. 152 and *passim*.

142. *not one jot or tittle*: This phrase, and 'Heaven and Earth shall pass away' later in the sentence, are adapted from Matthew 5:18: 'For verily I say unto you, Till heaven and earth pass, one jot or one tittle shall in no wise pass from the law,

till all be fulfilled'. Cf. also p. 58 above, 'Heaven and Earth shall pass away, but not one Tittle of *his Word* shall fall to the Ground'.

143. *not one word has fallen to the ground*: see 1 Samuel 3:19, 'And Samuel grew, and the LORD was with him, and did let none of his words fall to the ground'.

144. *No Impeachment of the Wisdom of God*: see the *History and Reality of Apparitions,* in *Satire, Fantasy and Writings on the Supernatural*, vol. 8, p. 251, where Providence is said to be able to do such and such 'without any Impeachment of its Wisdom or its Power'; cf. also p. 240, where to maintain so and so is 'an evident Impeachment of the Power and Justice, as well as the Wisdom of Providence'.

145. *We are told ... our Duty*: from the title of ch. 2 of Tindal's *Christianity as Old as the Creation*, p. 11.

146. *But what is all this to*: i.e. 'how is all this relevant to', a frequent idiom in *Applebee's Journal*, e.g. 23 November 1723, 3 October 1724, 16 January 1725, in Lee, *Daniel Defoe*, vol. 3, pp. 209, 312, 356.

147. *a jealous God*: See Exodus 20:5.

148. *visiting his Creatures*: inflicting punishment or vengeance upon them, a usage frequent in the Old Testament.

149. *hearing ... their loud Imprecations*: See the *Serious Reflections*, in *Novels*, vol. 3, p. 188: 'from what Hand come the frequent Instances of severe Judgment, following rash and hellish Imprecations? when Men call for God's Judgment; and Providence, or Justice, rather obeys the Summons and comes at their call: A Man calls God to Witness to an Untruth, and wishes himself struck dumb, blind, or dead if it is not true; and is struck dumb, blind, or dead'.

150. *Every Age is full of Examples ... Divine Justice has struck dead the perjur'd Wretches that have call'd God to witness to a Lye*: See *A New Family Instructor*, in *Religious and Didactic Writings*, vol. 3, p. 206, 'not to run into History, we have frequent Examples ... before our Eyes; here was one, the other Day, that affirming a Thing he knew to be false, wish'd he might drop down dead immediately if it was not true, and immediately he sunk down and died ... A Man giving a false Evidence in one of our Courts of Justice, as soon as the Clerk had express'd the Words, *So help you God*, and the Man kiss'd the Book, he fell down dead'.

151. *pursuing the Murtherer, often bringing him even to detect himself, and be the Instrument of his own Punishment*: See p. 60 above, 'the guilty Soul ... has no Rest Night or Day, till he even detects himself'. For Defoe's view that those 'guilty of any atrocious Villany' are often 'oblig'd to Discover it' themselves through a 'Necessity of Nature', see the parallel passages from *Moll Flanders*, the *History and Reality of Apparitions,* the *Review, Jure Divino*, and the youthful 'Historical Collecions' cited on pp. xvii–xviii above. On the self-betrayal of the guilty, cf. also *Applebee's Journal*, 2 March 1723: 'in cases of Treason, Murther, and the like Crimes, how often have we seen, that when the Guilty Persons have apply'd themselves ... to conceal their Guilt ... they have ... been their own Betrayers, discover'd the Crime, and detected themselves'. In these passages, to

'detect' means 'to expose (a person) by divulging his secrets or making known his guilt or crime; to inform against, accuse', for which the *OED* (2.a) cites no work later than 1645.

152. *frequent Examples, where the Crime has been seen in the very Punishment*: In addition to the passages from the *Serious Reflections*, the *Family Instructor II*, the *Commentator, Religious Courtship*, the *Political History of the Devil*, and the *Review*, cited on p. xviii above, see *The Present State of the Parties in Great Britain: Particularly An Enquiry into the State of the Dissenters in England* (1712), pp. 13, 334: 'they may read their Sin in their Punishment', 'a Man's Sin is sometimes read in his Punishment'.

153. *these Men lay a Snare for their own Souls*: The idiom is Biblical (Isaiah 29:21), and common in the period in figurative uses; cf. *Robinson Crusoe*, in *Novels*, vol. 1, p. 68; the *Political History of the Devil*, in *Satire, Fantasy and Writings on the Supernatural*, vol. 6, p. 97; the *Complete English Tradesman I*, in *Religious and Didactic Writings*, vol. 7, p. 166.

154. *plead his infinite Goodness in arrest of Judgment*: 'To move or plead in Arrest of Judgment, is to shew cause why Judgment should be stay'd, though there be a Verdict in the Case' (Cowell, *A Law Dictionary*).

155. *it gives them a loose in ... the worst of Vices*: 'To give a loose to', a common phrase at the time, means 'to allow (a person) unrestrained freedom or laxity ... to free from restraint' (*OED* 3.b).

156. *Reason may be ... blinded, by the rage of Appetite*: See *Conjugal Lewdness*, in *Religious and Didactic Writings*, vol. 5, p. 184: WHEN the Appetite governs the Man, he breaks all the Fences, and leaps over all the Bars that Reason and Religion have fixed in his Way ... the Rage of the Appetite blinds the Eyes, and ... neither Reason, Religion or Reputation, are hardly allowed to give a Vote in the Case'.

157. *hurried down the stream of their Affections*: In addition to the passages from the *Serious Reflections, Conjugal Lewdness, Farther Adventures,* and the *Political History of the Devil* cited on p. xviii above, see *Mere Nature Delineated*, in *Writings on Travel, Discovery and History*, vol. 5, p. 181, where Defoe asks 'why does Meer Nature ... hurry the Soul down the Stream of his Affections ... to what is gross, sordid, and brutish'.

158. *demonstration of Fact, against which it is to no purpose to argue*: See *A New Family Instructor*, in *Religious and Didactic Writings*, vol. 3, pp. 205–6: 'To argue against Reason is unreasonable, but to argue against Fact is impracticable; 'tis not to be done; Reason may be doubted and question'd, but Facts are Matters of Evidence, and undeniable; Demonstration is above Argument; when the Matter of Fact is brought out and set in open Light, all Argument is at an End ... the Rulers and Elders of old ... had not a Word to say where Fact appear'd: *We cannot deny it*, say they, *we cannot argue against Demonstration*, it is not to be done'.

159. *to raze out the fear of God from the Minds of Men*: See the passages from the *Political History of the Devil*, *A System of Magick*, and the *Commentator* cited on pp. xviii–xix above.

160. *leave every Man to walk in his own Ways*: See Acts 14:16, [God] 'in times past suffered all nations to walk in their own ways'.

161. *no King in Israel … right in his own Eyes*: See Judges 17:6, 'In those days there was no king in Israel, but every man did that which was right in his own eyes' (cf. also Judges 21:25); cited in the *History and Reality of Apparitions*, in *Satire, Fantasy and Writings on the Supernatural*, vol. 8, p. 117. With this paragraph compare the following passage from the *Serious Reflections*, in *Novels*, vol. 3, p. 118:

> no Method can be so direct to prepare People for all Sorts of Wickedness, as to perswade them out of a Belief of any supreme Power to restrain them; make a man once cease to believe a God, and he has nothing left to limit his Appetite but meer Philosophy; if there is no supreme Judicature, he must be his own Judge and his own Law, and will be so; the Notion of Hell, Devil, and Infernal Spirits are empty Things, and have nothing of Terror in them, if the Belief of a Power superior to them be obliterated.

162. *Fear of God … is the Beginning of all Religious Wisdom*: See Proverbs 9:10, 'The fear of the LORD is the beginning of wisdom'.

163. *erecting his Goodness … above all his Name*: an ironic paraphrase of Psalm 138:2, 'thou hast magnified thy word above all thy name'.

164. *search the Scriptures … whether these things are so*: See Acts 17:11. I cannot identify 'the noble *Berozar*', but the name probably has something to do with Berea. In this town in Greece, the Jews to whom St Paul was preaching are said in the present verse to be '*more noble* than those in Thessalonica, in that they received the word with all readiness of mind, and searched the scriptures daily, whether those things were so' (italics added).

165. *the Foundation of God standeth sure*: 2 Timothy 2:19.

166. *We trust this is a Building which is of God, and shall for ever stand*: Probably an echo of 2 Corinthians 5:1, 'we know that … we have a building of God, an house not made with hands, eternal in the heavens'.

167. *Heaven and Earth … to the Ground*: See Matthew 5:18.

168. *If it should so fall out … when their Mistakes appear*: On the appearance of these lines in *The Storm*, in *The Storm. An Essay*, in the *Political History of the Devil*, and (twice) in the *Serious Reflections* – where Defoe uses them, as they are used here, to clinch the case for the Pascalian wager – see pp. xii, xxix–xx above.

169. *act according to the Gust of your own Desires*: See the passages quoted from the *Serious Reflections*, *Conjugal Lewdness*, the *Family Instructor I*, the *Family Instructor II*, and *Moll Flanders*, p. xix above; see also 'this Gust of their greedy Appetite' in *A New Voyage Round the World*, in *Novels*, vol. 10, p. 239.

170. *Hand of God ... stretched out against such things*: The phrase echoes a series of passages in Isaiah, beginning with 5:25, in which 'the anger of the LORD [is] kindled against his people, and he hath stretched forth his hand against them'.

171. *the vindictive attribute of God* [repeated two paragraphs later]: See p. xix above, where the phrase 'vindictive attribute' is noted as occurring in the *Serious Reflections* but perhaps nowhere else. In modern usage the adjective usually has pejorative connotations ('given to revenge; having a revengeful disposition', *OED* 1), and did so even at the time: thus Jeremy Collier deplores 'a vindictive Temper', declaring that 'Vindictiveness is an uncredible Quality, and argues a little Mind' (see 'A Moral Essay upon Revenge', in *Essays upon several Moral Subjects, Part III*, 3rd edn (1720), p. 34). Yet 'vindictive' is evidently being used here in the neutral or favorable sense of *OED* 2, 'Involving retribution or punishment; punitive, retributive; avenging. Now *rare*'.

172. *who ever hardened himself against him and has prospered?*: Job 9:4.

173. *Would ... God ... suffer them to be swept away in a Pestilence by thousands, as by an overflowing Stream*: See *Due Preparations for the Plague* (1722), in *Writings on Travel, Discovery and History*, vol. 5, pp. 89, 126: 'a Pestilence sweeps whole Towns and Cities of People away, and Death rages like an overflowing Stream'; 'the Plague spread dreadfully ... and swept away the People like an overflowing Stream'.

174. *cast his Fear behind your Back*: Variants of this phrase, expressing disregard or disdain for something, occur in the Old Testament: at Ezekiel 23:35, God reproaches Jerusalem, 'thou hast forgotten me, and cast me behind thy back'; at 1 Kings 14:9, God upbraids Jeroboam, 'thou hast gone and made thee other gods, and molten images, to provoke me to anger, and hast cast me behind thy back'.

TEXTUAL NOTES

The British Library has three copies of the original 1730 edition. One (699.d.13. (1.)) has the half-title but lacks the first and last leaf of the final gathering (G1 and [G8]); it is bound as the first in a volume of seven 'Religious Tracts 1730–2', all responses to *Christianity as Old as the Creation*. The two other copies (4014.f.7. and 109.b.27.) have the complete text but lack the half-title. 109.b.27. was reproduced in 1995 as an ESTC microfilm, which later became the ECCO version; this has served as copy text for the present edition. Microfilming cut off margins with loss of letters and/or punctuation on pp. 11, 12, 29 and 30; here these have been supplied directly from the printed edition. Its collation is [*1], (B-G)^8; in other words, the title page is a separate leaf. In the original edition there are printer's ornaments at pp. [1] [B1^{recto}], 51 [E2^{recto}], 86 [G3^{verso}], and 95 [G8^{recto}], but their source has not been identified. There were no later editions.

Other copies are located by ESTC or WorldCat at Emmanuel College, Trinity College and the University Library, Cambridge; at the Bodleian Library, Oxford; and in the United States at the libraries of Brigham Young University; Iliff School of Theology; Trinity College; University of Pennsylvania; and Duke University (2 copies). Although a half-title is present in the Brigham Young and one British Library copy, in all others it is either missing or not recorded.

In my treatment of the text, I have followed the policy established by Furbank and Owens for the Pickering & Chatto edition of Defoe's writings, and have used the same method of indicating textual emendations by a superscript letter. The original is on the whole well printed; all intentional departures from it are listed here. The 1730 punctuation is somewhat erratic, but has been altered only in three passages, as noted, where it seriously obscures or distorts the meaning apparently intended.

In the 1730 edition, Chapters 4, 5 and 6 were misnumbered 3, 4 and 5. In the Eighteenth Century, manuscripts were sometimes entrusted to more than one printer for the sake of speed, and if Chapter 4 had begun a new gathering (e.g. signature E), this practice might have seemed a plausible explanation for the present errors. But the new (misnumbered) chapter in fact begins on [D5^{recto}], and the catchwords are continuous throughout, so mistakes by a single printer appear to be responsible.

In the following list, the emended reading in the present edition precedes the 1730 reading.

12   Luke xxiv. 45] Luke xxvii. 44
15   so the Fact should be deny'd,] so the Fact, should be deny'd,
16   Objects, but ... Nature; he] Objects; but ... Nature, he
25   Excursions] Excusions
27   Heb. xi. 4] Heb. xi. 3
29   CHAP. IV.] CHAP. III.
33   Religion of Jesus] Religion of of Jesus
35   CHAP. V.] CHAP. IV.
38   Gen. iii. 15] Gen. iii. 13
43   CHAP. VI.] CHAP. V.
44   for that Reason alone] for that Reason above
46   1 Tim. i. 15] 1 Tim. i. 13
47   its] their
49   CHAP. VII.] CHAP. VI.
57   things, and] things? and